Faith Before Faithfulness

Faith Before Faithfulness
Centering the Inclusive Church

H. William Gregory

The Pilgrim Press
Cleveland, Ohio

The Pilgrim Press, Cleveland, Ohio 44115
© 1992 by the Pilgrim Press

Printed in the United States of America
The paper used in this publication is acid free and meets the minimum requirements of American National Standard for Information Sciences— Permanence of Paper for Printed Library Materials, ANSI Z39.48-1984

97 96 95 94 93 92   5 4 3 2 1

Library of Congress Cataloging-in-Publication Data

Gregory, H. William (Harry William), 1935–
     Faith before faithfulness : centering the inclusive church /
   H. William Gregory.
       p.   cm.
     Includes bibliographical references and index.
     ISBN 0-8298-0930-9 (alk. paper)
       1. Church renewal.   2. Conversion.   3. Spiritual life.   I. Title.
   BV600.2.G74   1992
   262'.001'7—dc20   92-31718
                                                                    CIP

To the church and, in particular, the churches that have allowed me the privilege to serve with and to them as an ordained member of their staff:

The Claremont Congregational Church, UCC
Claremont, California

The First Parish in Lincoln, UCC, UUA
Lincoln, Massachusetts

The First Congregational Church of Berkeley, UCC
Berkeley, California

The Woodfords Congregational Church, UCC
Portland, Maine

Contents

Contents

Acknowledgments

As an ordained minister who serves in the local church I am indebted to each and all with whom and for whom I have served. The trust, challenge, support, affection, and accountability provided me have helped me grow and benefitted our common service in the name and spirit of Jesus.

With regard to the writing of this book I am particularly indebted to The First Parish in Lincoln and First Congregational Church, Berkeley, for sabbatical time during which the reflection, research, and writing that culminated in this book was centered.

The good help and encouragement of Ansley Coe Throckmorton and the editorial skills and patience of Harold Twiss and Barbara Withers have been significant to me and helpful in the realization of this work.

Finally, to Cordelia Jacobs, my friend and secretary at First Congregational, Berkeley, who has given countless hours of ready and efficient reading, word processing, and copying, I express my genuine thanks. Without her I doubt that this book would be a reality.

SECTION I

Mainline Churches:
Where We Were,
Where We Are,
Where We Need to Go

CHAPTER 1

Redefining Ourselves

> For radical monotheism the value-center is neither closed society nor the principle of such a society but the principle of being itself; its reference is to no one reality among the many but to One beyond all the many, whence all the many derive their being, and by participation in which they exist.
>
> —H. Richard Niebuhr
> *Radical Monotheism and Western Culture*[1]

This is a book written from the trenches of American Christianity, the local church. It is the product of the struggle shared with my lay and clergy colleagues in many churches but particularly those of the inclusive wing of Protestantism, which were known as mainline churches during the first two-thirds of the twentieth century. Since the mid-1960s these churches have known institutional decline. In recent years we who are these churches have been struggling to understand this decline, gain inspiration for relevance and vitality, find guidance for program, action, and goals, and discover a definition for success that is not dependent upon numbers alone. Presented in the first section of this book is an analysis of where we in inclusive Christianity are in the 1990s, how we got here, and where we need to be in order to be faithful to God's calling to our future. The second section expands specific components of the spiritual life of members of these mainline churches, referred to in this book as inclusive evangelicals. The chapters of this section are designed to help the reader and local church programs expand the horizons of reality from the world

3

view of the Enlightenment to the God-centered world view of the Bible.

Describing churches as exclusive or inclusive is based upon whether the dominant understanding within that church is that God's way and will for humankind is revealed exclusively through Jesus Christ or, inclusively, not only through Jesus Christ but also to some degree in other religious traditions and human experience.

Through analysis of our church and its time it is my conclusion that what is needed in our inclusive churches is conversion. The conversion of which I speak is of ourselves, our church's members, and those seekers who find their way to our churches. It is a conversion from a highly individualistic world view that encourages self-centeredness and works righteousness, a world view encouraged by the Enlightenment's emphasis on the worth of the independent and rationality-dominated mind and heart. It is a conversion to belief in God as the foundation of reality. It is belief in God at center whose essence is grace, whose goal for creation is right relationship ordered by love, who is the central force for justice. It is belief in God of whom Jesus taught and whose will and Christ Spirit were given human form in the life of Jesus. It is belief in God at center, the foundation of creation, who was, is, and will ever be. It is belief in God who calls humanity to follow God's initiative to just relationship with God, neighbor, and self. It is our belief that God, as the forgiving parent of the prodigal child, waits for our return to the home of love where we all began and for which we long.

The God to whom we must return, who is the source and initiator of all justice and hope, in whose affection all true joy is known, dwells in mystery, in large measure beyond rationality's reach. A world view with the God of dynamic grace at center will honor and cultivate the capacities of mind and spirit that meet and are met by truth encountered in the mystery of God. A Christian world view should not disdain rationality but also should not be based upon rationality as the ultimate scale of reality. The Christian world view is founded upon the truth of God's grace, which is centered in mystery—the mystery to and through which we are led by the Holy Spirit's inspiration of our imaginations, beyond rationality's control.

The Appendix offers a course outline for the use of this book in local congregations. The goal of the course is the members' growth in the trust and love of God, neighbor, and self for the purposes of (1) encouraging and/or supporting conversions to belief in the God of Jesus Christ as the undergirding reality of existence, and (2) encouraging and supporting the hearing of God's call to our individual and collective ministries and following it.

It is the experience of the grace of God that is central to conversion and the nurturing of faithful living. This grace exists at the center of reality and requires the whole of one's being to experience and understand. Most of us have been raised to measure reality with rational analysis of sensory perceptions. This is using only a portion of our brain. There is far more to reality than rationality can comprehend. Religion acknowledges a reality broader and deeper than intellect can explain and calls for faith in more than can be weighed, timed, or measured. Religion calls for the involvement of the whole self—body, soul, and mind—with all of its rational and intuitive capabilities. Religious truth is poetry and algebra, music and words, mystery and measurements. Conversion is necessary for movement into the fuller world of religious reality. It is a conversion from faith in a reality defined by rationality with humanity in control to faith in a limitless world explored by intuition, imagination, and reason with God in control. In this world view rationality aids us by defining and manipulating the truths experienced through intuition and imagination. Rationality is not the measure of reality but a tool for its exploration. Intuition is not the proof of reality but the vehicle that opens us far beyond ourselves and to God, by whose grace we are called to our fullest being and worth.

Inclusive Christians Are Losing Their Faith Identity

Sometime in the twentieth century many American inclusive churches lost track of their central faith identity. I am convinced that it was the consequence of two interdependent developments: (1) the acceptance of a world view based upon faith in individual rationality to define and control reality that excludes mystery, and (2) a growing assumption of religious and cultural symbiosis and even unity. This led us to affirm the values of culture as reflections of, or perhaps identical to, our basic religious values. But school prayer was eliminated in deference to individual rights. Release time from public school classes for local churches to do religious education was discontinued. Inclusive respect for religious differences muted our faith claims in favor of affirming the values of other faiths, religious or secular. Less frequent church attendance undercut what meager Christian education was being offered children and adults. Secular and inclusive Christian values and faith objects were enmeshed, their differences becoming unclear.

Each generation must choose to believe if faith is to survive. Faith must be claimed and defined by the life and words of believers. It will be different from other ways to live and believe. If persons are to choose to believe, be converted, it will be as a consequence of this definition.

Conversion Is God's Yearning and Ours

A classic debate in the church, particularly in Protestantism, revolves around whether conversion happens to the believer or if the believer chooses to believe and thus is converted. Central to the discussion is the question of human free will on the one hand and the irresistibility of God's grace on the other. Convoluted concepts arguing for or against predestination emerged from these considerations. The understanding that forms the basis of this book is that conversion results when an individual chooses to say yes to the unrelenting call of God to order our lives around God's mind and heart. The call is sounded in experiences of the power and beauty of grace, experiences showing the consequence of both its presence and absence. With Augustine I understand that God has made us for God's purposes and that we are restless, ill at ease, dis-eased, until we find our rest in God. That finding is a consequence of God's yearning and our own, being consummated in an embrace such as the prodigal son and his father knew upon the son's repentant return. Yearning is not conversion. Choosing to embrace is its beginning. Entering the embrace freely is the "yes" that confirms one's willingness to be converted. Knowing the embrace is conversion's consummation, the beginning of faithfulness.

Conversion in this age involves believing in God as the center of existence, the foundation of reality. It is believing without abandoning the facts about the natural order continually uncovered by human reason and imagination in the practice of scientific investigation and experimentation. A case in point is the theory of

6

evolution. Christians on the exclusive end of the spectrum of Protestant thought argue against evolution in an understandable but mistaken effort to claim the biblical world view as truth, basing it on scientific fact rather than as religious insight. They are correct in their effort to claim the truth of the biblical world view but in error as they use the rigid category of rationality to explain the truth of the myth and symbols of our religious literature. This approach suggests that the answer to the challenge of secularism is to deny the truth of Enlightenment discoveries.

Unless inclusive Christians choose to abandon evangelism to more strident and narrow visions of the faith we must learn how to proclaim the gospel articulating a God-centered world view that affirms and integrates the gifts of Enlightenment-affirmed rationality. At the same time we must affirm an understanding of truth that reaches beyond facts and any one doctrinal proclamation. The fullest truth of God is found in the use of rationality that values and ultimately defers to intuition and imaginative open-endedness in its encounter with the mystery in which most of God's reality dwells. The call of God to believe and center one's life around the grace-filled way and justice-seeking will of the "One beyond all the many, whence all the many derive their being, and by participation in which they exist"[2] comes to us from this mystery and meets us in our imagination.

Inclusive Evangelicals

A gift of inclusive Christian thought is that in its respect for rationality and individual freedom it is open to the truth of other faiths, traditions, and academic disciplines. But, respecting differences and individual freedom, it has been uncomfortable with evangelism. I am convinced that we who are inclusive must rediscover and reclaim our revivalist roots without abandoning our openness. Inclusive Christianity must understand the need for conversion. When we do we will insist upon being called evangelicals, inclusive evangelicals.

A dilemma for us who are in the inclusive wing of Protestantism, who have been in the mainline but are no longer there, has been what to call ourselves in our new circumstances. It must be a label that is true to our understanding of God and God's call to us for our unique servanthood. It needs to hold on to what we have been and reflects what we are called to be. In this book I will encourage those who have called themselves or have been called liberal to think of themselves as inclusive evangelicals. This is in contrast to individuals and churches on the exclusive end of the theological spectrum, which in this book I will call exclusive evangelicals.

Inclusive evangelicals will hold on to the vision of inclusive Christianity, its tolerance, the freedom of thought and expression it respects, its dedication to the dignity of all persons and their innate right to justice. Incorporating the word *evangelical* is done with the recognition of the history of its roots in European Protestantism. It is also chosen to affirm our need to proclaim the good news of God's grace so that others will know conversion to belief in and lives of service to the compassionate Creator God of Jesus Christ at center.

Out of the Mainstream

In *A Religious History of the American People*, Sydney Ahlstrom[3] looks to the late nineteenth century and calls the Presbyterians, Disciples of Christ, Congregationalists, Methodists, and Baptists the "evangelical mainstream" of America. What these denominations had in common, in large measure, were their Calvinist roots, revivalism, and Arminianism with its doctrine of the free will response of individuals to God's grace and its belief that Christ died for all people, not just an elect. Conversion was the goal of their gospel proclamation.

It is not clear if Ahlstrom identifies the denominations referred to as "mainstream" in the mid-1800s as being so within Christendom or within American culture. I suspect that it was in both. Today it can be argued that these churches are not in the mainstream or mainline of American Christianity. They are certainly not, nor should they be, champions of the mainstream of American culture. (By mainline I mean the churches with the most recognized influence upon the country's religious self-image.) We inclusive evangelicals have our place in society but it is not as America's culture-affirming churches. This is an observation rather than a lament, one that sets the course for faithfulness and new life in our churches. Our goal should not be to become mainline or mainstream once more but to become clear in our Christian identity and faithful in our life and mission.

Whatever form and function the churches of Ahlstrom's evangelical mainstream will assume in this new time will be determined in God's providence. We are not called to be the mainline church or the sideline church. We are called to be believers following as closely as we can the way we find God leading. The first and continuing task of faithfulness is to know and love God as the ultimate and central reality, the heartbeat of existence upon which all life—the life of heart, mind and soul; the life of societies, cultures and institutions; the life of Earth and all creation—depend. Integral to this task is telling others of this truth through words and deeds so that they too can accept and live out of this reality for the benefit of their life, the life of God's world, and the glory of God. This is the evangelism we must undertake, the consequences of which will be the conversion of minds, hearts, and souls to a living faith in God at the center of reality, who was in Christ reconciling the world to the God self.

CHAPTER 2

An Overview of Decline

> In the new religious environment (in the United States), liberal Protestantism is a minority voice and one player among many in a more truly pluralistic modern context. Thus, while conservative Protestantism is facing new internal tensions owning to its new position closer to the center of American life, liberal Protestantism faces its own crisis of identity and purpose from a position closer to the margin.
>
> —Wade Clark Roof
> William McKinney
> *American Mainline Religion*[1]

As the churches of inclusive Protestantism have been declining in recent years, no small attention has been paid to the contrasting increase in numbers of members and dollars found in conservative and fundamentalist congregations across the U.S. Whatever our sisters and brothers on the theological right of organized Christian religion were doing seemed to be working, and whatever the sisters and brothers on the left—and even in the center—were doing didn't, if numbers were the measure. And numbers definitely are a measure. Surveys, analyses, commentary, hypotheses were generated by most every mainline denomination and foundation. The sum of their conclusions said "the decline is not all your fault." It was some comfort to the thousands of clergy struggling to make a success of their ministries. The findings legitimized new conceptions of what it might mean to be successful even if numbers continued to decline.

People were not leaving the inclusive churches in great numbers to go to exclusive, i.e., fundamentalist or conservative, congregations. In fact, those who moved that way were more than offset by members of the churches on the right moving into churches on their left. Yet while the churches on the right grew, those on the left became smaller. What was happening? For one thing, new members in the growing churches were coming from the significant population growth of the nation, one that made the decline in liberal churches even more pronounced. But the population growth was happening in a segment of the population that was not in the inclusive churches. Inclusive Protestant families' birth rate, 1.5 offsprings per family, is the lowest of families in institutional churches. In addition to this, those children born into inclusive Protestant families were not staying in the church.

These dynamics are pointed to as a part of what has come to be called the "back door loss" of our churches, membership loss into nonchurch status rather than some other sector of organized religion. Back door loss was the consequence partly of the young people of the mainline Protestant churches not continuing in the churches of their childhood as well as the loss of adult members, some to other churches, most into nonchurch status.

Young people of the sixties were the children of the post–World War II era, the baby boom. The combination of their numbers in adolescence in the sixties and seventies with the dominating idealism of adolescence and the exposure to the shadowy side of American life—materialism, racism, militarism, and sexism in particular—had powerful cultural ramifications. It all led to a generational cynicism regarding the nation, its professed values, and its major institutions. Institutions such as the church and the university, advertised to be embodiments of the highest values in the culture, were particularly susceptible to charges of impurity and hypocrisy. Young people not involved in the church had little incentive to become a part of it.

In the inclusive churches, the young people who remained active were often encouraged by their clergy and leaders in their criticism of the churches to which they belonged. Rather than stay in the churches to affect renewal, which was what their church leaders hoped for, most of these young people opted out after graduation. Adult loss out the front and back doors is attributed by some to a falling away of persons disagreeing with the political

11

orientation of the leadership of the inclusive mainline churches. These churches championed human rights of minority groups, challenged the foreign policies of the nation, and questioned the consequences of its economic system. Some studies suggest that this was not a major drain of inclusive church members, that those who remained in these churches did so in part because of the concern and involvement in justice issues that had become an integral aspect of their church's life.[2]

Turmoil Itself Contributes to Decline

Over the past twenty-five years, however, whatever presence of turmoil resulted in inclusive churches over involvement with social issues was often more unsettling than the specifics of the turmoil. In a real sense, an unwritten covenant of culture affirmation to which members agreed when joining a mainline congregation in the late 1940s and 1950s was being broken by the role these same churches, and to a greater degree their denominational leaders, were assuming in their position as culture critical in the 1960s and 1970s. With the breaking of this covenant, an understanding of the theology that informed any new covenant of membership needed to be established. Much of the inclusive church leadership at that time was prepared to lead in matters of justice but was neither well prepared nor disposed to lead in matters of the Spirit and theological interpretation.

On a more pragmatic level, there was the simple fact that turmoil precluded peacefulness in congregational life. Given the pace of life in our modern world, it is reasonable that persons joining a church would do so with the expectation that there would be some degree of sanctuary, some portion of the peace that passes all understanding to be found in the fellowship of believers. This is true today and has been true over the past twenty-five years. The fact that turmoil, rather than peace, was the dominant state of affairs to be found in most churches on the inclusive wing of Christianity over the past twenty-five years cannot help but be a factor in some adults leaving these churches. Some exited through the back door to nonchurch status, others through the front door in search of congregations more compatible with their politics or at least more dedicated to peaceful coexistence with the nation's policies and practices.

A major contribution to the turmoil in my opinion is that the inclusive churches had not, and perhaps still have not, learned to practice the inclusiveness, the pluralism, the democracy they preached. Having found our identity before the 1960s as churches affirming the presumed undergirding values of the prevailing culture we had little or no experience as outsiders, as minorities, as the unheard. A friend of mine who identifies herself as an outsider told me, "Those of you on the inside cannot see nor hear those of us on the outside until we hurt you." Insiders' blindness and deafness to the voices, perspectives, and values of different ones on the outside plague all majority peoples just as it plagued our mainline churches.

The prophetic voices in our churches spoke on behalf of the outsiders but often did so with little time for persons on the inside with opinions and perspectives contrary to theirs. Similarly, sad to say, in the distress of controversy in the churches in recent time (perhaps it has always been this way for insiders and outsiders), the insiders being challenged seldom found time or respect for those who challenged them. Even churches whose polity is congregational and should know that there is truth and correction to be found in contrary opinions were distressed by the controversy of differing opinions.

After a period of struggling with differences without learning to value outsider perspectives a controversy fatigue sets in where the slightest distress is upsetting. In such a setting the tension necessary for creativity is unwelcome. This happens in local congregations as well as in denominations.

It would appear that denominations assume that a clear voice, uncluttered with contrary opinions, speaks truth the loudest. Thus denominational pronouncements are made that appear to those outside the church as if all members are speaking with one voice. Within the churches these pronouncements are seen either to be speaking to the churches and lacking adequate mechanisms for response or speaking for all the churches and lacking adequate mechanisms to include the diverse opinions therein. Either way the message in the medium is that diversity is neither welcomed nor considered an adequate conduit for truth.

Difference will always generate some degree of turmoil—differences of opinion, differences of background, race, or culture, for example. Certainly theological differences have and do generate turmoil in congregational life. Now that we are no longer the mainline churches we will be in a position to learn more easily the value of minority opinions and perspectives because ours is a minority opinion. If we can accept the fact that we are not mainline we will be aided in the lesson to be learned from the truth found in diversity.

The Churches and Culture in the Twentieth Century

During much of the twentieth century most mainline Protestant churches have defended the innate values of American culture. We have been culture-affirming with our function within culture being to hold our nation and communities accountable to fulfill the promise of the Constitution and the Bill of Rights. This was understood as the same as holding true to the country's "Christian" values. The culture and the churches were secure in the assumption that they stood together for God and "the American way."

When one joined a mainline church, little if any time was given to defining and celebrating the content of the prospective new member's faith; seldom was one's faith identity differentiated from cultural identity. Spiritual longings and genuine needs for community were acknowledged, and assurances to new members that these needs would be met were given. Correlation between their satisfaction and the church's role in pursuing justice in the public realm were often vague but affirmed as part of the church's role in maintaining the honor and viability of American culture.

This assumption of partnership with culture is at the center of a struggle within inclusive Protestantism, which has been going on throughout the twentieth century. Whereas local churches assumed their function to be primarily the monitoring of the values of their local communities, they understood that they had a role in the nation as well. In both settings the church was to see that cultural behavior reflected the Christian values of the founding forebears.

At the outset of the century a literary voice of inclusive Protestantism named itself the Christian Century. This was to be the century when the culture would become all that God intended it to be, inclusive Protestant Christian. The social gospel of Walter Rauschenbusch dominated the prophetic vision of the early century and was fanned by the stress of the Great Depression of the

1930s. The Second World War dominated energies in the forties. The fifties saw spectacular growth of mainline church numbers as the culture and the mainline churches worked together to establish a new era of peace and prosperity. As late as the early 1960s seminarians were reading Gibson Winter, who in his book *The New Creation as Metropolis*, called for the Christianization, albeit a secular/religious amalgam, of culture. Winter's plea was for the church to work toward a fully just society,[3] devoid of denominations and religious congregations. In the spirit of inclusive Protestantism Harvey Cox wrote *The Secular City*[4] in praise of humanizing values to be found in secular society. It seemed the stage was set for the transformation of the secular culture to some higher level of existence where the religiously enlightened in its midst, for example, mainline Protestants, would provide a yeasty presence resulting in a cultural bread of noble and new composition.

George Webber, identified at the time with the East Harlem Protestant Parish, wrote *God's Colony in Man's World*, which presented an alternative view of the proper place of the religious community.[5] Webber called the churches to their responsibilities in the secular culture as religious communities in but not of the world for God's purposes of renewal and redemption of the world.

Winter and Cox saw God working toward a day when the church gives up its life for God's purposes of renewal to forces of God already at work in the world. The church was called to recognize and affirm this work as God's and defer to it. Webber saw the church as the custodian of a vision and an understanding of God and God's purposes that the culture could not fully see or adequately value. For the church to defer to culture would be to abandon the vision.

The tension between the secular and the religious, between a God-centered world view of our biblical tradition and the Enlightenment-influenced self-centered world view of western culture, was at the heart of the debate of which Winter, Cox, and Webber were a part. My argument is on the side of Webber and challenges the assumption of much of twentieth-century inclusive Protestantism that culture and the church are partners in God's work.

It is not being argued that God is not at work in the world outside of the church. On the contrary, God is exerting influence in all aspects of life and has done so from the beginning. It is being argued that the church has a particular calling to mission dependent upon its experience of the grace of God at the center of existence and its faith in the embodiment of the grace of God in the life and teachings of Jesus. To define ourselves as culture affirming or culture critical reflects the cultural captivity of the mainline churches and misses the fundamental point that our identity is based upon our faith in the existence of God at the center of all reality and not our relationship to culture. We are to be God's colony in God's world for whatever purposes God will use us. When culture is transformed for God's purposes it will be God who transforms. We can be sure that our faithfulness to God will play a part in whatever transformation the compassion of God will accomplish, but we can also be sure that God and not the church will accomplish it.

Are the Theologically Inclusive Changing Places in the Culture with the Theologically Exclusive?

An interesting switch seems to have occurred in the past twenty-five years. The churches that were mainline are now sideline. Those churches that were outside culture's affirmation in the first half of the twentieth century are finding themselves inside. As sideliners we are outsiders and in a position to challenge the values of the culture with greater theological clarity. If we persist in ignoring our cultural captured identity, longing for the bygone days of mainline prominence rather than claiming our primary religious identity as followers of the God of the crucified Jesus, the resurrected Christ, we will continue to lose touch with the reality of the truth we are called to know and proclaim. Rather than being fools for Christ, which is our hope for life, we will be fools for Mammon, a god who kills fools. A line from Habakkuk defines our fate with Mammon as our god. Mammon's "greed is as wide as Sheol; like death he has never enough" (Hab. 2:5b). Those churches to the theological right that were openly countercultural are rapidly moving to the mainstream where they will no longer be able to identify themselves outside the culture but, as is happening, become its defenders. They also risk being co-opted by the values of Mammon. With their strong sense of identity built upon exclusive rather than inclusive attitudes, the theological right has always been easily nationalistic. Their patriotism is not new. Their taking on the ways of the culture is new. How did this turn of events transpire?

The place of the mainline Protestant churches in the cultural stream of the United States began changing in the 1960s. As has been discussed, the spirit of the age was captured by the idealism of the baby boomers in their adolescence. Many leaders in the mainline denominations took to this idealism with prophetic zeal. With the ethical issues of the Second World War clearly in mind and the life and theology of Dietrich Bonhoeffer affirming resistance to evil authorities, we were vulnerable to either/or thinking. We entered the new idealism of the 1960s as ducks to water. Now our faith was relevant; our cause was just. But our judgment was diminished by self-righteousness. We were hard pressed to see in ourselves racism, militarism, egoism, and sexism, let alone love others in whom we saw it. The truth is that we lacked the necessary humility and graciousness that is to be found in right relationship with God. Also lacking was sufficient wisdom concerning our own sinfulness, and God's saving ways of judgment and grace, discerned in honest theological inquiry.

The challenges to faith in the rational-secular world view of the Enlightenment and the perceived challenges to the authority of scripture suggested by biblical scholarship, which drew heavily upon academic practices dependent upon rationality for truth testing, had left us inclusive Protestants uneasy with the subjective aspects of our faith. We were anxious to be relevant in the real world. We were critical of other-worldly preoccupations of more pietistic approaches to Christian living. In other words, we were alive and responsive to the demands for justice in our land and embarrassed by what appeared, from our intellectual perspective, to be sentimental religion and fuzzy thinking. The traditional language of the faith seemed archaic and rigid. It came with the baggage of previous insider blindness. Spiritual quests were seen to be vulnerable to excess and self-indulgence. Finding our theological concepts and language at best marginally relevant and the mystical inclinations of the spiritual quest escapist, many Protestant clergy and leaders, certainly those on the inclusive wing, reveled in the relevance we discovered in our prophetic call.

The laity of the inclusive churches were slower to get with the program. As has been mentioned, they joined their churches covenanting to be a part of a culture-affirming congregation, a culture that was deeply invested in the radical individualism inspired by the Enlightenment but without the bonding into a faith community provided in previous ages by a shared faith grounded in transcendent mystery.

Following the Second World War, returning soldiers, sailors, and marines were anxious to get on with their lives, to establish families, find homes, be part of a secure life free from the threats of violence and poverty. Being part of a church fit that ideal well. People flooded the facilities. New churches had to be built. New members were brought in as if they were entering school, not expected to know much about the subjects taught when they entered. That would be taken care of in the process of congregational life. There was a great trust in the power of the preached word on the part of the clergy and the laity. Sunday morning sermons would fill biblical and theological voids in the minds and spirits of the congregations. But preaching seldom if ever converts one's world view and, in spite of some heroic efforts to do otherwise, preaching was and must be grounded in the literature of the faith, the collection of legends, the stories and history of lives shaped by mysterious grace that we call the Bible. If there is a shared world view between preacher and congregant, a major change of priorities in living can be brought about from the pulpit. New dimensions of understanding the subtleties of one's faith can be cultivated. But if the preacher speaks from a perspective upon reality that is foreign to the congregation, the words are not clearly heard, the concepts and contexts misunderstood.

Much of the preaching of the inclusive churches in the sixties and early seventies was grounded in the prophetic word of scripture, with its God-centered world view. The preachers/pastors in these churches longed for a way to show the faith relevant to the real world. But many in their congregations found themselves on a stormy sea of change without a rudder of an agreed-upon authority to guide them. They hadn't been asked to change their Enlightenment world view for the biblical world view. Without the authority of a shared transcendent vision of grace and justice for all peoples, born of knowledge and affirmation of God at center, the judgment and calls for change coming from their pulpits seemed reckless and relative rather than reasonable and relevant.

The prophetic call to the United States to change its unjust ways was sounded from most pulpits of inclusive Protestantism in one degree or another. The preachers worked to convert the entire culture but those to whom they spoke were the members of their own congregations. The ways that were being called unjust were ways that were considered acceptable, ignored, or unseen when most of the members joined their churches. They covenanted in membership and good standing in the eyes of God as loyal Americans, not critics of American ways. Church was thought of as a place for the positive reinforcement of existing values. Criticism felt negative, even unpatriotic. It is no wonder that turmoil resulted.

Growing from the Inside Out

What was and is needed first is conversion, conversion from a self-centered world view to a view of reality that experiences and believes in the gracious but Mammon-opposing God of Jesus Christ at its center. This is the biblical world view. To understand the nature and appropriateness of conversion in our inclusive churches, training in spiritual exercises and devotions in addition to intentional faith education must occur. When we learn how to help one another in our churches to experience God's grace and find the language from our tradition, aided but not dependent upon contemporary metaphors to express that truth, we will grow as persons of faith and as faith communities. This is growing from the inside out. Institutional growth will not be our primary preoccupation. Our purpose will be faithfulness to the God of grace found in scripture. Thus defined and committed we could expect our churches to be healthy.

The reality of God experienced in the mystery of grace needs to be made intelligible for purpose of articulation and communication. This is a task of biblical and theological education that our churches must undertake to help faith find understanding. It is more than just an interesting task for those so inclined. It is a vital task for the life of believers, the church, and God's world. Accomplishing it provides us with the language, thought forms, and symbols necessary to encourage and support the religious life and work of our churches. It gives us language with which we can be clear to our children about the faith tradition into which they were born and for which they, if they in their turn choose, will be responsible. It provides us with the conceptual base and language we need to enter conversation with seekers after faith, with other

19

Christians as well as seekers and believers not in our tradition. At the present time we in inclusive churches have little if any faith language in common, very little to use with one another, let alone others, to tell of our God, our Christ, our religious vision, its content, its hope and joy. In spite of what some skeptics may say, this is not because we are without a God, a gospel, a Christ, a call.

Walk the Walk and Talk the Talk

In the 1960s a legitimate criticism rose of liberals, many in the inclusive wing of the church, from leaders in the civil rights movement. We were accused of talking the talk but not walking the walk. We talked a good civil rights fight but seldom put our bodies where our mouths were. Leaders in the United Church of Christ and other mainline denominations heard the criticism and took it to heart. Talking the talk without walking the walk was hypocritical. Struggling at the time with our self-doubts about the relevance of organized religion, we were coming to face the degree to which we were captured by cultural values. Relieved that justice action gave us a way to be faithful, as we longed to be, we set ourselves to the task of walking the walk. Many of the creative, energetic, adventurous leaders of our churches called for and pursued a faithful walk with Jesus, the suffering servant, the man for others, by taking to the streets. Our leadership was involved in various significant causes and issues: community organization to alleviate poverty, standing and marching with our African American brothers and sisters to rid the nation of racism, protesting the war in Vietnam, working against sexism, later against homophobia. Each and every social evil and ill of which we were conscious was called out and opposed. We put ourselves and our churches on the line with pronouncements, funding, personnel, and encouragement of action by our local congregations. While we were trying to faithfully walk the walk, we overlooked the need to talk the talk of our faith. Our hope was that our faith would show through our walk. In the process we were losing our religious language.

Talk without the walk is hypocritical. In the church the walk without the talk of faith loses accountability to God. I am not speaking of the talk that is puffery, self-righteousness, empty rhetoric in the name of prophetic pronouncement. I am speaking of the talk in which the biblical word is given expression, talk of what we experience of God, of what our tradition has given us that we are called upon to continue, of what is faithfulness and to whom we are faithful. If we pray and serve in the name of Jesus who is our Christ, who is Jesus and what does it mean to name him as our Christ? What of the trinity, the Spirit, resurrection, redemption, judgment, freedom, forgiveness, liberation, eternal life, grace, truth, justice? What words do we use to tell the stories of our faith journeys? Do these ideas, these words have anything to do with our reality, our meaning, our purpose, our ministries, our dreams, our hopes? If we lose the ability to talk the talk we cannot speak of the sacred, the pearl of great price, that has been given to us in the faith and life of Jesus and passed down the tumultuous centuries through the minds, hearts, and lives of countless faithful witnesses to today.

The "Extravasation of the Sacred"

Phillip Hammond tells of another aspect of the inclusive church that puts our faith language in jeopardy.[6] In order not to offend those of different persuasions with whom we are in conversation we choose not to use words that identify us as separate from them. We are anxious to affirm similarities with others rather than differences. We search for words that affirm shared values and experiences, words that minimize alienation. For example, in conversation with Jewish friends or relatives I hesitate to mention the name of Jesus out of recognition of the great suffering that has been caused Jews in his name. Yet there is no name, no word that captures for me more of what I understand as the essence of the sacred, calling me to reverence and respect for others and God's creation, than the name Jesus. It is the Christ Spirit of Jesus that demands that I honor and respect the Jewish person with whom I am speaking. It is the Christ Spirit of Jesus that places me in fervent opposition to those who are anti-Semitic, who have persecuted Jews over the ages.

More than that, in many of our churches we find it uncomfortable to use the name of Jesus or talk God talk in conversation among ourselves. It's all right from the pulpit but seldom in our committee meetings or our social gatherings and hardly at all when we gather as friends outside the church building. It sounds too religious and doesn't seem to have a great deal to do with anything anyway. It suggests fundamentalism or some other narrow constriction of faith. We are finding ourselves without acceptable language from our Christian tradition to speak of our faith. We are more comfortable with the language of the new physics to speak of the mystery of divinity than the word symbols of our Christian tradition. We look to poetry and psychology for religious symbols more than to our Bible and the literature of Christian discourse from over the centuries. Most of us are more comfortable with the word symbols of other faiths than with our own. This is not a plea to abandon the metaphors from beyond our tradition to aid in understanding it. It is a plea to find ways to claim the metaphors of our Christian heritage and use them as illustration and illumination of the sacred truth they embody.

The consequence in our churches of our reticence, we who are church people, to use the language of our tradition is what Drummand calls the "extravasation of the sacred." It is a good choice of words for the phenomenon even if it is uncommon. *Extravasation* means seeping out or leaking. In medical use it refers to the improper loss of blood from vessels. Without a vocabulary of faith with which we are secure, we will be apologetic and deferential. We will assume that definition in and of itself is excluding, that the only way to be inclusive is to be wishy-washy. But the Jesus I name as Christ is not exclusive. The faith to which he leads me is Christian. That is who I am. What I believe as a Christian is not what all others who call themselves Christian believe, but that is no reason to abandon the language. In fact, it is all the more reason to explore it, define myself as a believer, and claim my tradition.

Growing from the inside out means legitimizing conversion and being intentional about faith education. In these ways we will strengthen the churches and their members in faith and faithfulness. Evangelism in these churches will be done by proclaiming what we know and experience in our time, the good news of God's graceful word and deeds in our lives.

The renewal that will come in our churches will not be at the cost of abandoning the prophetic word or witness. To the contrary, faithfulness to God at center and the Christ Spirit discovered there will provide the experience of grace that reveals our unity with all people. This is the foundation of the prophetic ministry. It is also the spirit that inspires the compassion that will enliven a loving faith community, one rejoicing in the grace of God and dedicated to talking the talk and walking the walk of God's love in God's world in our time.

CHAPTER 3

Finding Our Way

> Scarcely reminiscent of the earlier controversies be-
> tween modernists and fundamentalists, the new breed
> of liberalism was defined not so much by theological ori-
> entations as by support for direct action in the broader
> turmoil raised by the civil rights movement. And con-
> servatism came increasingly to be associated with the
> view, not that race relations should never change, but
> that direct action was too conflictual, too divisive, push-
> ing for short-term gains at the expense of religion's
> longer-term place in the social order.
>
> —Robert Wuthnow
> *The Restructuring of American Religion*[1]

Participating in churches such as those I have served is no longer
encouraged by the dominant cultural values in the parts of the
country I know the best, the West and the Northeast. People have
to explain to their friends why they would join a church. Spending one's time and resources in a religious institution sounds
to many like a sentence handed down from the court of parent-
al authority than a choice one would make freely. Even those
who claim to value religion personally or would argue that organized religion is a good influence on society find the press of earning a living, keeping relationships, and pursuing recreational
opportunities so demanding as to leave little time or resource to
invest in organized religion. This was not the case following
World War II. Times have changed, yet the buildings we occupy
and the memory of vital church life often harken back to those
days.

In recent years I have spent many hours with colleagues around the United States lamenting the pressure upon clergy and laity alike in mainline congregations. The distress is around the fact that in most of our churches numbers have been steadily decreasing since the mid-1960s. The clergy feel called upon by their members and their own sense of responsibility to do something about it. One hope of pastoral search committees from inclusive congregations since the mid–1960s is that the new minister will reverse the trend and increase membership.

Clergy in mainline churches from the mid-1960s through the 1980s have been caught in a double bind. One bind presses us to produce new members and new money for the health of the institutional life of the congregations, an institutional life often measured against the numbers and assumptions of the 1950s. The other bind is made up of pressures from the culture-challenging teachings of Jesus and from prophetic voices in our consciences, our Bibles, our seminaries, and our denominations. We are called to preach, teach, and demonstrate a gospel of grace and dignity for all people—an inclusive gospel. Integral to this gospel is a demand to call and work for justice for those within and outside the mainstream of American culture. This justice work challenges the secular values, the materialistic and individualistic goals of our culture. The good news thus proclaimed implies judgment upon and a call for significant change by those carried along and kept afloat by culture's secular mainstream. To some degree this is most of us who are in the churches that have been known as mainline Protestant. It takes a deep understanding of the faith to hear prophetic news as good news to those who have made peace with the cultural mainstream.

How many times have we preachers/pastors/prophets heard that our task is to comfort the afflicted and afflict the comfortable? That is a vulnerable position to be in when most of the comfortable we would afflict are either our employers or the logical candidates for swelling our rolls and budgets.

The "Yes" and the "No" of the Gospel

The gospel of Jesus Christ is a "yes" and a "no" at the same time, which can sound as if the preachers or lay persons holding forth are speaking out of both sides of their mouths at once. It is a "yes" to the worth of every person and all of creation. It is a "no" to each act and every system that diminishes and denies the worth of each person and all of the creation. To speak the yes and the no at once calls for deep grounding in God, a faith maintained in humility and kindness inspired by the compassionate Christ. To be able to hear the yes and no of the gospel calls for a tolerance for paradox, an opening to the mystery of grace. The secular mainstream of our day does not have an easy time with paradox. There is not much being taught in our schools or found in management training programs in our corporations to reinforce, for example, the truth of Jesus that to lose one's life for Christ's sake is to find it.

Dorothy Bass, a leading church historian, brings some comfort to the clergy and laity of churches that were once in the mainline but are now caught in the double bind of the yes and no gospel. She writes that the literature analyzing the decline of our churches leads her to "disencumber the churches of misunderstandings" about the reasons for declining membership. Her first disencumbering point is that "ministers and congregations are not failing when they fall short of the growth and participation expectations they inherited from the 1950s."[2] Times have changed and new standards for success in these churches are needed.

Having read the literature and worked in the vineyard of inclusive Protestantism since 1966, Bass's words ring true to me and are of some comfort. They will be comforting to most of the members of our congregations. To some of my members and colleagues, however, they will seem lame rationalizations for inadequate strategies, insufficient and misguided labor on the part of clergy and lay leadership in the declining churches.

The question underlying this debate is *What is success in churches that once were mainline but are no longer?* I am not ready to abandon the possibility of membership growth as a mark of congregational vitality. I cannot, however, condone membership growth as an end in itself, a strategy too often gained by speaking the yes of the gospel without speaking the no. In place of church growth but not in opposition to it I call for inclusive evangelism that begins with experience of and belief in God—whose being is filled with grace, whose will for creation is just and abundant life—at the center of reality, the foundation of existence. Inclusive evangelism springs from the belief in, experience of, and knowledge about the God of grace who was in Jesus Christ calling the world to right relationship with God, not from fear of diminishing numbers.

Success from the Inside Out

Success in our churches is harder to measure than membership. The success Jesus speaks of has to do with faithfulness to the just and loving God, the One in whom we live and move and have our being. Losing all for such a God is gaining. It is clear that secular society does not operate out of such a faith or world view.

Every Sunday many of us in what were mainline churches are confronted with empty pews that two or three decades ago, certainly within memory of many who still come to worship, were filled—or at least there was a reasonable expectation that they could be. The power of those symbols is not lost on anyone in attendance and is reinforced by reports of burgeoning attendance coming from crystal cathedrals, exclusive sanctuaries, fundamentalist and sect group gatherings.

In such a climate it is little wonder that there has been a ready market for books written about the growth of the exclusive churches as well as "how to" books written to the laity and clergy of what were mainline congregations about church growth. My own denomination, having taken church growth as one of its priorities, has been mailing a steady stream of excerpts from this latter literature to its member congregations. Using videotapes we can hear newly popular church-growth experts instruct us in the hows and whys of reaching new members and keeping them. Much of this literature can be helpful but too often it does not address the basic issues of conversion that we must address if we are going to grow as communities of faith. Based upon a strategy of growing from the outside in, it is designed to add members, increase attendance, and expand budgets by doing a better job of public relations. It talks about the importance of the parking lot, of easy access and plenty of good signs to help people find their way to the sanctuary, church school rooms, rest rooms, and so on. It counsels us about such things as effective advertising, welcoming visitors, following up on their visits, getting our members to invite their friends. It is helpful advice, and in a congregation I have served in Berkeley, California, we followed it. Those who know of my predecessors in the First Congregational Church of Berkeley, United Church of Christ pulpit understand that that congregation has known good preaching and competent leadership of laity and clergy alike over the years. Yet its numbers have gone down since the mid 1960s along with most everyone else's in churches of inclusive Protestantism. In such times survival may be a legitimate measure of success. The church growth strategy designed to grow from the outside in misses the basic point. At this time in the life of our culture and churches the growth that is needed begins with the growth of spirit, Christian identity, and mission—growth from the inside out. This calls for a redefinition of the relationship of our churches to our culture and a restatement of our mission based upon our primary identity as believers in God as revealed in Jesus, empowered by the Holy Spirit.

Our God-centered World View

A fundamental discrepancy in world views exists between the Christian faith and secular culture. Our secular world view, shaped by the Enlightenment, which was a liberating word in its time, centers upon human rationality, and as the goal of the successful ordered and ordering life, prizes control over one's self, others, and one's environment. Those of the Enlightenment believed faith in human rationality was the sword to slay the ignorance, superstition, and abuse of power of monarchs and clerics who ruled in the name of subjective truths, truths *they* defined. Religion of the Enlightenment put individuals near the center of their world, responsible only to God. This idea drove the Protestant Reformation. Increasingly monarchs, rulers, and clerics were granted authority by the free-will consent of the people. In the tradition of congregational polity, which epitomizes this movement, no individual stood between God and the believer. Over the succeeding centuries, as the pendulum of self-understanding swung toward individualism, faith in human abilities to know and control replaced faith in the traditions and mysteries of God. God, beyond rational definition or manipulation, was moved out of the center of reality. In place of a theocentric world view, Enlightenment logic led to an anthropocentric world view. In the logical extension of this world view each individual exists at the center of his or her reality. The God thought to exist elsewhere than at the center of reality is not the Holy One of Hebrew and Christian scriptures.

The God-centered world view of our biblical tradition does not deny human rationality and responsibility but understands humans to be responsible to God. God is ultimately responsible for the past, present, and future. God is God and we are not. Human beings are called to "see" God, discern God's ways, and seek to serve God's purposes. But rational capacities are not enough to open us to the reality that can be known of God. This book exists to say to the inclusive churches that the central tasks before us today are to know God, to love God, and to live lives based upon God's being the core and foundation of reality. This is our unique calling and task. It sets us at odds with the prevailing culture. It does not abandon reason but instead recognizes that reason alone will not strip our eyes of secular blindness. The pendulum has begun to swing back toward valuing the mystery in which humans "see through a glass darkly." The view through this glass does not reveal all, but we do see. And, in the midst of our less than absolute clarity, we are given a way, by the grace of God, a way to be and do. Our way is Jesus Christ.

Religious awareness, using intuitive and rational capabilities, sees the sacredness of persons and things. Intuitive skills open us to the mystery. The experience of mystery and perception of the sacred are central to a God-centered world view. Mystery, where the greater part of the sacred dwells, is beyond rationality. The sacred, although capable of being perceived by persons of all world views, becomes a road sign to the source of all that is sacred for religious people. We theistic ones name that source God, the One in and by whom we find our being, hope, and meaning. Rational skills are used to define and tell what can be told of the experience of the sacred, but in its fullest dimensions, it is beyond telling.

To the person operating out of a self-centered world view the sacred is also recognized intuitively and rationally. Their intuitive perception leads toward mystery but is usually challenged by a dominant rationality that measures reality in categories that the human mind and tools can control. Thus mystery is diminished in or denied worth all together. The agnostic plea is often heard at this point: "It may be that there is reality beyond what I can know, but not being able to perceive it with one's rational perception and manipulate it, I cannot address or concern myself with it."

From the perspective of one choosing to define reality from a religious world view provided by Christianity, the self-centered perspective is blind to crucial understanding about human existence. It misses life's purpose and meaning without the expanded "seeing" provided by the experience of God, who was in Christ, who is at the center of all. God is experienced prior to rational interpretation and provides meaning and purpose beyond but not exclusive of rational understanding.

It is the premise of this discussion that what was the mainline Protestant church is losing its grip upon mystery and the sacred. With the loss of this hold it is also losing its passion and a religious language with which to speak of the mystery and sacredness of God and all of God's creation. Losing its religious grip leads to unfaithfulness. Losing its passion leads to blandness. Losing its language leads to silence. As we have served as our culture's main churches we have worked hard to find language and deeds that would speak to our culture of Christ and God's ways. In the process we have chosen neutral language so as not to offend those we respect of different persuasions. Often we sought metaphors based upon existent cultural perceptions of reality. In this process the cultural world view becomes the base reference, a reference not large enough for God. In such a way we have been co-opted to a large degree by the world view of the culture to which we have intended to bring good news based upon a quite different world view. If co-opted totally, we will lose the essential gifts that the inclusive evangelical churches of Christendom have to give to our culture and the world.

The Gifts of Inclusive Christianity

A primary gift inclusive Christianity has had to give is the embodiment of a religious vision that has the humility to recognize that we have truth but not all the truth, that we are part of God's purpose on earth but not the whole of God's people. We recognize and value diversity in the creation as an integral part of the Divine intent. We hear God's call to be for the fullest realization of each person rather than for compliance of each to an ecclesiastical or ideological norm. We seek unity in our diversity through faithfulness to the one God whom none of us can define, who can be best spoken of through the testimony of all of us.

We have done well affirming the intellectual integrity of each believer and fostered rational inquiry concerning our Bible, our theologies, and religious history. But scholarship does not reveal God. It can bring balance to our understanding of expressions of previous experiences of God. It can also encourage trust and offer analysis of contemporary spiritual experience. We have embraced the Enlightenment honoring of rationality and will do well to continue to ask that spiritual experience stand the examination of rational inquiry. But we are learning that rational inquiry is not the final test of truth and thus need to let the mystery of spiritual experience call us to new levels of knowing God. We have too easily dismissed such testimony as irrational.

Another gift inclusive Christianity has to give is kindness born of faith in and experience of the compassionate God of Jesus, who, in the phrase describing Dietrich Bonhoeffer's understanding of Jesus, he followed God and became "the man for others."[3] A vision of lives of servanthood springs from this gift, a vision organized around a passion kindness spawns, a passion for justice for all peoples, a justice always in tension with the prideful aspirations we find in ourselves and at the heart of secular culture.

I would like to think that another gift inclusive Christianity has provided the larger church has been humor, particularly an ability to laugh at ourselves when we take ourselves too seriously. That has dwindled considerably as we have become champions of justice without the humility upon which mystery insists. I am still pleased, however, when someone comes out of a worship service of which I have been a part saying that they didn't realize that it was all right to laugh in church.

Incorporating the gifts of inclusive Christianity with the clear need for the churches to encourage conversion to a God-centered understanding of reality leads me to rename us. We are inclusive evangelicals.

Conversion

The renewal of what was the mainline Protestant church calls for a strategy based upon religious conversion. Without abandoning the gifts of reason, independence, measurement, and manipulation made available by the Enlightenment, it must be recognized that the self-centered world view the Enlightenment spawned is fatally flawed and will not save humanity or the creation. Unless it recognizes God at center it will destroy both. At the same time we need to recognize that the self-centered world view is the primary world view not only of our culture but of many, if not most of us who are church members. If we are to be faithful to our God and our Christian heritage a conversion to a God-centered world view within our churches, as well as of others into our churches, is necessary. It is a conversion because a major, life-changing, altering of one's understanding of self and the world is involved. It is Christian conversion because it happens as the result of an individual experience in Christian community of the unfathomable but immanent grace of God revealed and offered in Jesus Christ.

A good deal of this material is presented with the hope that it will aid the local church in its work to encourage conversion. The consequence of this conversion will be the increase of passion and compassion in the life, worship, and mission of our churches. Our mission will flow from compassion born of the encounter with the Spirit of the crucified and resurrected Christ who embodies the grace of the God we worship. We will more clearly recognize ourselves as the body of Christ in the broken world that God calls us to serve. More often recognized as followers of Jesus, we will shy from the identity of Christian less frequently and be able to talk the talk of faith as well as walk the walk more easily.

Strategies for growth in churches that do not recognize the basic need for conversion are fighting fire with kerosene. To the degree that they succeed they will be building bigger and better secular humanist organizations. There is a place in our pluralistic society for such organizations, but that is not the primary work of Christ's church. It is certainly not the work to which God is calling us with the vision of our being inclusive evangelical churches.

CHAPTER 4

On Conversion

True decidedness is not of doctrine, but of life orientation. It is a commitment of life, thoroughly, wholly, in
every department and without reserve, to the Inner
Guide. It is not a tense and reluctant decidedness, an
hysterical assertiveness. It is a joyful and quiet displace-
ment of life from its old center in the self, and a glad and
irrevocable replacement of the whole of life in a new
and divine Center.

—Thomas Kelley
The Eternal Promise[1]

Being "born again" is a religious concept abandoned by most inclusive Christians but continued and embraced by our exclusive
evangelical sisters and brothers. And most who would identify
themselves as inclusive Christians are content to let them keep it.
Being "born again" seems to mean narrow definitions of priva-
tized grace, rigid doctrinal formulas for salvation, convictions that
others must become replicas of the saved in a grand homogeneous
company of act-alike, look-alike, think-alike sweet and smiling
psalm singers.

If that is what conversion means, then count me out, too. I
doubt that many of our "born again" brothers and sisters would
see themselves in that picture either but it is close to the stereo-
type we inclusive Christians carry of those converted ones who
call themselves born again. Without trying to define what conversion means to others I would rather talk about what it means to
me, to us who I call inclusive Christians who might be willing to

call ourselves inclusive evangelicals. The first thing I am sure of is that each individual, each generation, must accept the faith as theirs or the faith dies to them. With the tide of secularism rising around us, with more and more children growing up with little or no exposure to the Bible or to being a part of a community of faith, with schools forbidden to pray, leisure-time activities eroding sabbath practice, televised religion trading in an individualism/consumer mentality based more on image and entertainment than mystery and relationship, the churches that were mainline cannot count upon the culture to guide people into their life or to confront them with the tenets of the faith with which we can help them wrestle. We must "feed the sheep," spread the word, evangelize if we hope to have people in our churches in the years to come.

Is Conversion the Word to Use?

One clergy friend suggested that I would do better in communicating my meaning if I abandoned the word *conversion* and spoke of *converting*—that we are in a constant process of change, of converting from one stage to another, from one level of understanding to another. Another colleague called my attention to a word with deep spiritual roots in New England Congregationalism, *awakening*. Perhaps I should not call for conversion but for awakening. I like how awakening feels. It suggests a new morning, rising from a sleep of unawareness. It also suggests that we are awake to our real condition, that what was known during sleep was distorted and illusionary. My experience of conversion has these aspects to it. But would the word work? Would it communicate the combination of revelation and choice of which conversion speaks?

Another thing about the word *conversion* that appeals to me has to do with being born again, a concept I don't want to give over completely to exclusive evangelicals. It is a birth and a naming that is brought about by revelation, often found in the mystic experience. In the case of Christian conversion it is a revelation of grace, coming from beyond one's self and nurtured in the church, that results in one's knowing God and the way of God, knowing that one is known, accepted, and called to servanthood by God. As birth is natural, the consequence of the essential order and creativity of existence, so being born again is a spiritual metaphor for

Christian conversion, a natural response to the essential grace and continuing creativity of the author of existence.

Then, related to birth, there is the naming. Are we called by name by God and in hearing the voice recognize the speaker, as Mary Magdalene did in John's account (John 20:16) of her encounter with the risen Jesus outside the empty tomb? Or are we born again and finding ourselves in our new world named as are American Indian youth after the ordeal of initiation into adulthood? In conversion it is God who names us by calling our name. Whether as Mary Magdalene or as the newly named Indian youth we know a new reality in hearing our name as if for the first time. This time the speaking of the name is an expression of unconditional acceptance and affirmation. We are free to be who we are for God's purposes, which is our fullest joy.

Being born again works as a description of conversion also because to be converted is to start with a new perspective, from a new place. The words that suggest gradual process and change, such as *converting*, are right as they call our attention to the fact that conversions are not made out of whole cloth, that we were someplace on a path before we found ourselves in a new place on a path. Conversion does not mean discounting what has led up to it. Who can say that all previous steps were anything but necessary to bring us to our present place? Conversion does mean that in all directions one looks, after the experience of seeing and choosing, things are in a new light and seen differently than they were before.

Conversion is often spoken of as being saved. I find myself in agreement with those who speak of life's spiritual journey as a series of conversions, that it is not a once-and-for-all experience. At the same time I think I understand why many Christians find truth in their belief that one is not saved before conversion, yet after conversion one is saved once and for all. Saved from what? From the hellish consequences for individuals and all peoples when a self-centered world view blinds us to the recognition, understanding, motivation to love and justice, and subsequent hope discovered in faith in the gracious God of Jesus Christ at center.

Life Set in a New Direction

Two paths diverge in a wood, as Robert Frost tells us, and the one we choose makes all the difference. The crossroad that calls for choice may be a high religious understanding or mystical insight. It could be inspired by the example of other lives who have chosen the higher way. Perhaps in the fervor of a religious service you become convinced of the need to center your life in God.

Whatever the circumstance in which the decision to believe in God at center is made, it is the culmination of God's continual encouragement of you to choose life that prompts the decision. Still, it is not God's encouragement that completes your conversion but your choice. Conversion means choosing. You choose to believe God is God and seek to live your life in right relationship with the One Jesus knew as the fountain of compassion, lover of justice, forgiving Creator. The choice, with its implied commitment, makes all the difference.

The Path of Light

Choosing to believe that God is at the center, is the foundation of life, is choosing to follow the way of God, the path of light. The path, revealed with an enlightening experience, is chosen in preference to a darker way. It leads to summits of greater light, clearer seeing. Yet the path of light has its dark turns and bewildering experiences as it moves on from conversion to expanded understanding. Once one has known the amazing grace of God, he or she will still experience dark nights of the soul and may cry as Jesus did from the cross, "Why have I been forsaken?" But the basic understanding that God exists at the center of reality and that God's dominant nature is grace will not be forgotten. It will be challenged from beyond and within one's self but it will not be forgotten. It will be the North Star for all of life's navigations.

New opportunities that amount to conversion appear frequently along the way after the initial revelation and choice. Additional forks in the road appear to those who choose the path of light and to those who inadvertently (can one consciously choose hellish circumstances?) choose the lower path of semiblindness, the path of self-sufficiency and personal control.

Those who have chosen the way of semiblindness will encounter other forks in the course of their journey. One branch again leads toward God's light. Once more a choice is made and the journey continued. Each choice along the path of semiblindness makes all the difference because it is a choice for living in the darkness of self-absorption or in the fuller light of the gracious God that shines from the center of existence.

It is possible for one who chooses the faith in the gracious God, progenitor of Jesus Christ, to refuse to move along a new fork encountered on the path of light. For example, a fork calling for liberation for some sisters and/or brothers may be refused because the difference being addressed between the believer and the ones seeking liberation has heretofore been thought unacceptable in the believer's mind. Conversion does not rid us of fear and the longing to be in control. It continues us on our journey empowered by faith in the revealed grace of God at center, but the journey to greater light and seeing is a lifetime adventure. The path being offered not only leads to the liberation of the oppressed but to the further liberation of the believer. The choice may or may not be another conversion and may or may not continue growth in grace, but it isn't the primary conversion.

Choosing not to follow where the liberating Spirit of Jesus leads diminishes the believer's understanding of God's grace but does not preclude it. Along the way there will be other forks in the path, one leading to new understanding of light; the other, chosen because of pride, fear, or self-deception leads back toward the black hole of self-centeredness. Even if the lower path is chosen we will never completely escape the power and influence of the revelation of the ultimate power of God's grace. It is an article of biblical faith that once we move from being "no people" to being "God's people" we are always God's people. This has to do with an indelible knowing, as a consequence of conversion, whose people we are. This has to do with God's faithfulness in the covenant made when we choose to believe in the God of Jesus Christ at center. It is not a matter of our earning or deserving to be kept from the pit.

Conversion is Radically Life-Changing

The breakthrough of intuitive and rational understanding about God, one's self, and all others that comes when you are seized by grace; when you choose to believe that you are loved by God; that by the heartbeat of existence you count; that life makes sense even though evil, tragedy, and absurdity are integrally in the mix—this breakthrough, this conversion, this seeing is radically life-changing. It is radical because it is God centered and not self-centered. It is radical because you come to know that the most important thing is not that you love God but that God loves you unconditionally. It is radical because you not only know that God loves you and accepts you as you have always, deeper than you have known, wanted to be accepted, but that God loves all others with the same open-hearted intense compassion. From this knowing, which is beyond rationality and is the basis for all subsequent logic about humanity and creation, flows the truth and passion that undergirds the believer's love of justice, kindness in relationships, vision of community, practice of devotion.

It is accurate to speak of this salvation in terms of eternal life. When "the light of the knowledge of the glory of God in the face of Christ" (2 Cor. 4:6b) is seen and chosen as the illumination of faith for one's life journey, it never goes out of memory or present moment. Where I part company with many who are inclined to speak of their eternal life as opposed to others' damnation is that I cannot find a hint, a speck, a glimmer of truth in the premise that this God of amazing grace that I have come to know would be indifferent to, let alone damn to eternal punishment, those who don't know God in this way. God provides various paths to reveal divine grace within and besides the Christian way. Others may in fact be on a path of darkness but God does not, will not abandon them. New paths to light will always be provided throughout eternity. I understand and believe in eternal life. There are, in my mind, those who would seem to deserve eternal damnation. When my mind is illuminated by the mind of Christ it serves no purpose other than self-justification to believe in anything other than God's grace as the fundamental reality, a reality that does not include eternal punishment.

Paradox in Conversion

A paradox in conversion is that one is changed once and for all yet never ceases to change. The life lived with the gracious God at center is a sequence of changes that come as the result of new understanding. There will be awakenings, consciousness raising, additional revelations. New vision will be gained and/or given that does not contradict the converting illumination but expands it. When one is converted to the God of Grace, known in Jesus Christ, one is changed once and for all in a way that will not be changed. Yet being open to change, to new seeing along the path, is an integral part of living in grace. Trust, not rigidity, marks the will of those converted by grace.

The conversion of which I speak is a paradox in another way. It is believing in spite of unbelief. Faith is not without doubt. Faith is living as if reality is as the experience of grace says it is. It is an intuitive knowing argued against by some rational observations and supported by others. Faith needs imagination to understand and create its metaphors. It is not an easy way to live in a world that writes off what it doesn't understand as "only imagination." Conversion leads to faith with conviction but not with unmitigated certainty. This is another way in which an inclusive evangelical understanding of conversion is different from what others may think of when they speak of their or others' conversion. Doubt is an appropriate aspect of humility, and we are humbled when grace finds us. When you come to believe in the existence of and know the experience of the full acceptance of you by the One whose essence is eternal love, acceptance based upon your being rather than anything you have, can, or will do, when you know in your heart that although you are in some ways alone you are at the same time never completely alone because the gracious love of God includes you in its boundless compassion, then you are appropriately humbled. Doubt, as an aspect of this humility, has shadows in which fear still dwells. Fear is there because doubt signals the lack of one's control. It is doubt based upon the recognition that what is is more than you can know. What you know is profound but partial.

Conversion is not a completion of the journey. It is the major faith decision, the significant direction change along the way of discovery. Much that is unknown remains in the shadows beyond our vision and on the path ahead.

Our inclusive churches are full of people who have had conversion experiences and have not been given the language, encouragement, or opportunity to tell of them. We need to find ways to facilitate readiness to receive God's gracious spirit so that its members as well as others who would come to the churches in their spiritual search will believe that there is a God at the center of reality and that the nature of this God is resurrecting grace. Part of this process will be working to find ways to encourage those in our congregations who have had conversion experiences to speak of them.

Conversion Does Not Mean Abandoning the Enlightenment

As I have pondered the need for Christian conversion and sought ways to encourage it, it has come to me that the conversion I look for in the parishioners and parishes I have served is not a matter of condemning the Enlightenment world view in favor of a God-centered world view. It is a matter of bridge building from one to the other. I don't expect people to abandon the faith structures of definition, understanding, and measurement they have used to make sense and give meaning to their lives before they find sense and meaning in another faith structure. Any world view is a matter of faith whether it sees God at center or not. It is my experience and observation that lives work significantly better with faith in the God of grace at their center, but lives also work with other faith systems in place. Like Paul in Athens, we do better to affirm the religious dimension of all lives and point beyond idols to the One God suggesting a direction for the continuation of people's spiritual quest. This does not mean we are to affirm the worth of the lesser deities or defer from prophetic challenges of the consequences of living life dedicated to idols of control and self-serving. It does mean that each person is recognized to be a seeker after meaning, love, and truth. In our local churches we must meet people where they are on their spiritual journeys, help them to understand that they are on these journeys, and encourage them in the direction of conversion that will open their eyes to a new way, a God-centered way of seeing reality. Believing that God is at the center of all reality does not change the atomic table or invalidate the gift of artists and poets who claim not to believe in God. Rather it takes the believer beyond self-centeredness and puts the tools and insights of material manipulation to better purposes, purposes of life guided by faith in the essential life-giver.

A Debt to the Exclusive Evangelicals

I am speaking primarily of and to the people and churches of inclusive Christianity. But I am talking of conversion and being born again. I am talking about being a religious minority in a secular society. Some may be asking if I am not really a closet fundamentalist in the sheep's clothing of ordination in an inclusive denomination. I even get passionate about God. No, in spite of using some words and concepts not too often spoken of in our inclusive churches, I am an out-and-out card-carrying inclusive Christian. There is much about what I am writing that will be seconded by brothers and sisters who identify themselves as exclusive. I suspect, however, that my tolerance of other faiths and ways within Christendom is beyond the limits of many on the theological right. Yet, although I find myself very uncomfortable with most of what I know of fundamentalism in particular and much of what I know of exclusive Christianity in general, they are sisters and brothers in Christ and I have learned from them in ways that have not only perplexed my spirit but blessed it. To give expression to my thanks for the blessings I have composed a short letter to the churches of exclusive Christianity. It is composed to speak to whomever may read it from that segment of the faith as well as those within inclusive Christianity to understand my debt to exclusive Christians.

Dear Brothers and Sisters,

My primary purpose in writing is to acknowledge a debt to you. It was you who had the courage, and/or arrogance, and/or humility, and/or intensity, and/or dedication, certainly faithfulness, to present Jesus to me in my youth with sufficient clarity that I had to make a choice. My inclusive church was too timid to force the decision. It was at a weekend snow camp in Southern Californian mountains. I had gone along on a Young Life retreat because I was new in town, a senior in high school in need of friends and, although I wasn't aware of it yet, religion. It was good fun, playing in the snow with plenty of girls to share toboggan rides down runs sufficiently dangerous to encourage holding on tightly. Then the dues were to be paid. After dinner on Saturday we all had to listen to a man talking about Jesus. There was plenty of singing, mostly songs with religious words I didn't understand. But the songs were simple and spirited. It was fun to sing together. As the talk began I listened with half an ear. He caught my attention when he began talking about Jesus being alone in the crowd. Jesus could have been as lonely as someone moving into a new town in his senior year because his father had been transferred. Then the speaker began describing the crucifixion. It was a slow, painful death. Each nail slowly pierced, then plunged through his flesh as it was deliberately pounded through the hands and feet of this innocent man. "No one stood up for him!" the speaker turned-evangelist cried. "No one stood up for him. He was alone in his dying. Alone! Is there anyone here who would stand up for him? Raise your hand." My hand shot up with a mind of its own, but I agreed with it. "Good. Now will those whose hands are up [there were six to eight of us out of the group of forty or so] stand up?" What could I do? I stood, a little less confident than my hand had been but knowing that I would not, could not leave Jesus knowing how wounded and alone he was. "Thank you, you may sit down." That was easier than I expected. The meeting drew quickly to a close much to my somewhat embarrassed relief.

As we were filing out of the room one of the college-age leaders approached me. "I noticed that you stood up for Jesus. Would you like to learn something more about him?" What could I say? We found privacy in the front seat of someone's pickup truck. My companion pulled out a pocket-sized Bible. As we talked he quoted disjointed scripture and then asked, "Would you like to have eternal life?" That was a question out of the blue. It didn't' seem to have anything to do with what had gone on in the evening up to now but it was interesting. "I suppose so. Doesn't everyone?" "Yes, and here is how you get it. You say to Jesus, 'Come into my life as Lord and Savior.' " "That's it? that's all you do? If I say those words out loud once my whole future in eternity is determined?" "Yes, that's all you have to do. It says so here in . . . " He quoted a few scripture passages with which I couldn't argue, not knowing enough to try. But it didn't seem right to me. It was more like magic words than what Jesus and I had going earlier in the evening. But I said the words. A combination of not wanting to disappoint my self-appointed tutor and thinking, *What have I got to lose?* did the trick.

The next morning, on my way to breakfast, I was swarmed over by a group of young men who were very happy that I had eternal life. It was clear to me that I was in. I belonged. I was a Christian, a member of their club. Their enthusiasm and the easy affection extended this new recruit felt good and I accepted it. In time it passed. What remained was the recognition that Jesus lived and died in a way that differed from other ways, a way I chose and still choose to follow.

Back home I was assigned another tutor who set up weekly meetings with me after school. He was trying to get me to memorize scripture. It seemed that being a Christian meant memorizing scripture. I quickly grew tired of that and we parted ways. But I had entered a new way of looking at the world and my faith. Back in my Congregational church the hymns started making sense. My friend Jesus had a story that I began to learn. The more I learned, the more my instinct about eternal life seemed sound. Jesus was more interested in saving others than saving himself. I had the clear impression that concern with one's eternal life was self-centered and that Jesus wasn't. Jesus was God-centered.

Jesus is more to me now than a friend but there is still some of that in our relationship. I have the distinct impression that on that night on a snow-covered mountain, Jesus looked down from his cross and said, "Thank you, friend. Thank you for standing." I have dedicated brothers and sisters in Christ who hold a theology that I didn't, and don't today agree with, to thank for the introduction. As best I can I am still standing.

The unity that coordinates diversity is grounded in the experience and knowledge of the grace of God, the spiritual pillar. In our day a bridge between the Enlightenment world view and a God-centered world view is needed to facilitate that experience and knowledge. The next two chapters address the nature of that bridge, while Section 2 presents progressing steps across the bridge.

CHAPTER 5

Pluralistic Community:
A Paradox of Diversity in Unity

> For as in one body we have many members, and not all
> the members have the same function, so we, who are
> many, are one body in Christ, and individually we are
> members one of another.
>
> —Rom. 12:4–5

The differences that exist within us and between us need not be
denied. They are, in fact, the very stuff out of which God's new
creation is brought forth. To deny the differences actually diminishes the truth that God would have us know for purposes of our
faithfulness and God's continuing creation.

Perfection, completion, and invulnerability do not exist in the
real world and are not desirable goals. Pluralism, change, and finitude are the experience of all creatures in existence. God's peace
that passes all understanding comes to us as we find the faith to
live with this reality rather than escape it. There is a resolution of
contrasting and conflicting opinions and circumstances that results in peace. It is the peace that the revelation of truth in paradox provides. It is the peace given when we give up our need to
define and control and find ourselves held in the reconciling love
of the One in whom all things are one.

This is an essential part of the Christian gospel, the good
news of God's grace. Every part of us, our shadow and our light,
can be used for God's creative and graceful purposes. Denial and
defensiveness are not necessary. The goal of the religious life is
faithfulness in the midst of our complexity, not perfection that

eliminates complexity. This is good news because none of us is perfect, nor can any of us ever be. We are made whole, not pure, in God's judging, forgiving, reconciling, resurrecting love. The refinement of our natures does not burn sin or finitude from our minds and souls. It turns them to good purpose through God's loving forgiveness and our humble acceptance of this transforming grace. Finitude acknowledged becomes the humility that makes room within us to recognize value in others and admit to them how much we need them. The more open we are to God's grace, the deeper our humility. The deeper our humility, the wider the circle that we draw to include others in our affection and recognized interdependence. Within the forgiving grace of God vulnerabilities acknowledged, sins confessed, needs admitted become the openness and empathy that turn our wounds to instruments of understanding, acceptance, and healing of others.

Pluralism, multiplicity is the nature of things. Every one of us is radically pluralistic, with different and opposing forces in tension. It is the basis of our functioning. Coordinated, this tension is the source of our power, possibility, and future. It works this way in our bodies. The muscles are designed to work against one another or they don't work at all. Our nervous system runs on energy that is composed of positive and negative charges pulling and pushing in order to create the dynamic that lets them function. The body is constantly being built up and, at the same time, torn down. Birth and death are dynamic and need one another for their meaning. Personality and character are developed from the tension that exists between loss and gain. Pain is necessary for perspective. Our psyches are dynamos of conflicting interests, appetites, and motivations. We understand the apostle Paul when he says, "I do not understand my actions, for what I do not do what I want, but I do the very thing I hate" (Rom. 7:15).

Pluralistic Congregations

We are diverse and pluralistic, as are our congregations. We can rejoice in the effect of push and pull in our muscles, but the push and pull of differences of opinions in our congregations seems another matter. Even if we know that open and clear articulation of conflicting opinions and goals is necessary to realize the gift that each has to give the other, it is still hard work. There is a deep vulnerability that lives in all of us that can be activated when someone disagrees with, or worse, is angry with or plain doesn't like us. It is easier if everyone agrees. It seems more "Christian," happier. But if the agreement is bought at the price of honest expression of feelings or opinion, even if that opinion is an ambiguous one, it is not worth the cost. It subverts authentic community; it subverts faith. Authentic community is found beyond what Scott Peck, a psychiatrist whose lectures and books bridge psychology and religion, calls pseudo-community, the appearance of community where mixed emotions are hidden in feigned good will.[1] Faith in the purposes of God, who created the diversity in the first place and speaks the gospel of grace through Jesus, is subverted when our honest differences cannot be acknowledged and worked through. But again, it is hard work. Peck helps us understand the process. To get beyond pseudo-community, honest differences must be faced. This leads to chaos. All hell can break loose, or at least threaten to. Everybody claiming his or her right to be who they are seems to deny the right of those different from them to be who they are. Such denial is the opposite of grace, and the opposite of grace is chaos. It is grace that coordinates difference. Peck says that there are two ways to get out of chaos: organization or emptiness. Emptiness being too frightening, most of our churches choose organization. Emptiness is the acknowledgement of our powerlessness. Organization can cool the chaos, but as an answer to difference, precluding honest engagement, it does not lead to community. Organization uses its parts. Community honors them.

The path to authentic community leads through emptiness. Authentic community is grace, but it is costly grace. It is losing yourself to find yourself. If members of a group can confess to one another their powerlessness and the dreaded fear of worthlessness it prompts within them, they will have reached the necessary humility that opens them to see the gift that each is to the other. They are gifts by virtue of their differences as well as their shared humanity and hopes. When we find someone or some others who can value us for the things we have in common as well as for those we do not, when we can find people who will value us in spite of and even because of our vulnerabilities and weaknesses as well as our strengths, we are hard pressed not to love them. This is the beginning of authentic community.

Authentic community is experienced in many churches but seldom in an entire church. More often it is in a smaller group within a church. That is one reason small groups need to be encouraged in our churches. In smaller groups authentic community can be experienced and modeled in the life of the congregation. Everyone in a congregation has the right to be in community, to learn from experience the joy and power of true belonging. As more and more people in the life of a congregation experience the taste of grace found in authentic community, the whole life of the congregation moves toward its realization.

Can Worship Be Authentic Community?

Worship is the closest most of us come to experiencing community with the majority of the people in our congregations. It is there that we confess our common sinfulness and together receive forgiving grace. But if these experiences of confession and forgiveness are not happening in the church outside of worship, it is unlikely that liturgy alone can generate the life-changing impact of grace found in true community. Worship in our congregations is not pseudo-community, as Peck describes it, but is has some of its characteristics. Often it is people coming together who want to be kind and accepting with one another but have not found ways to be open about their negative feelings. Paradoxically this leads churches to be proficient in criticism. They are consciously or unconsciously restrained from the clear and full affection born in openness. Worship in most of our churches allows for mouthing of words that are neither understood nor experienced by all participants and smack of pseudo-community. But worship in our congregations is more than pseudo-community because the Spirit of God is always present.

As ragtag a group as we are, when we come to worship in our small-, large-, medium-sized buildings, in our formal, informal, semiformal styles, in our well-planned, unplanned services, with guitars and/or organs, applause or silent response, in urban, mid-urban, suburban, rural settings, with preaching that is superb or less, with vision that is sometimes clear and most times not, when two or three, or two or three hundred of us are gathered in Christ's name, the enlivening Spirit of God is with us. Life and death are faced and the power of God's love is proclaimed. Our sanctuaries have been impregnated with hymns and tears, laughter and prayers, blessed with deep commitments made between brides and grooms, between congregations and parents of baptized children, between congregations and their new members, between congregations and clergy covenanting to minister together, between congregations, clergy, and candidates being newly ordained. It is there that we have memorialized our dead and baptized our children. It is there that the word of God is read and interpreted, the gospel proclaimed. We have and do face our emptiness on occasion even if we are not fully comfortable speaking of it to one another. We can and have found ourselves in the presence of the mystery of the mighty and merciful God who loves us even if we are embarrassed by the passion it evokes. We do hear the demand of God that we do justice, which thunders in scripture and in the cries of the suffering amongst and around us that echo in our prayers and sermons. We are a people of God, a community of faith when we worship, more than pseudo-community. A test of the extent to which we have moved beyond pseudo-community to true community in our churches exists, measured by the degree to which differences of perspective and opinion are respected and valued.

Facing Difference for Deeper Unity

My experience of churches by and large is that we all have been taught to live most of our lives on the surface. We seem to have an inordinate fear of the differences we will find when we go a bit deeper with one another. It is as if the unity that undergirds us is too weak to withstand the pain of rejection we will receive if we are fully present, without the defenses of disguise and withholding. And maybe it is. Maybe the unity we affirm is a faith that we do not fully embrace—all the more reason for conversion to belief in God-at-center and the experience of God's grace as the sustaining reality of our lives. The grace that is the essence of existence is no weak thing. It has withstood all that the world has thrown against it, and still resurrection is its truth and compassion its enduring characteristic. A people's ability to be honest with each other, not hiding their differences from themselves or the world, is a clear mark of the strength of their faith. As we deepen our faith and clarify its content we will not only be recognized as those Christians who love one another, but even more significantly as those Christians who are honest with and still love one another. And those of us within such communities will know that it is precisely because we have learned how to accept the many contrasting and sometimes conflicting differences between us that we love one another all the more as we affirm our differences, similarities, and common faith.

The Blessing and Burden of Pluralism in the Inclusive Church

The pluralism of the inclusive church is a blessing and a burden. It is a blessing not only because of the many gifts and perspectives the various members can provide from their uniqueness but also because as the covenant community affirms and celebrates the differences in its midst, it gives concrete demonstration to the good news of the gospel that each is valued and a gift to all. It is a blessing as well to the whole church and to the whole of humankind as it demonstrates that a religious community can be open to diversity, affirming of difference. There is an innate humility and good will in that attitude that reflects the grace of God and provides hope for community between peoples of difference around the world.

Pluralism is a burden in part because not only does it take a great deal of energy to recognize and affirm our variety, but the freedom that sets the context in which diversity is encouraged can become an end in itself. Freedom as an end in itself lacks the obligation to move beyond diversity to covenant. Freedom has worth in the realm of God only when it is freedom for God's purposes. It is a gift of God that allows us choice, gives us responsibility, and provides the dignity of being partners with God in creation—very junior partners, but partners nonetheless. When the freedom that affirms our diversity is also used to build the covenant community, then God's purposes for the church are being pursued. Here independence is given up for a recognized interdependence. Covenant is the expression of interdependence. It is the interdependence of the people of God with one another and the interdependence of the people of God and God at one and the same time. Covenant is a promise made in which God and the people of God are interdependent participants in the ongoing work of justice, mercy, and loving kindness.

I shudder when forming the words that say God is in some degree interdependent with us. I shudder for God's self-imposed vulnerability, having chosen us as partners in covenant, and I shudder at the audacity of the claim. But it is not my claim. It is Jesus' claim, his good news captured in the simple but profound pronouncement that God loves us. That being the truth, then we indeed have effect upon God based on the need that love entails. There is never any doubt of our dependence upon God. It is another dimension of our understanding of the grace of God to recognize that God chooses freely to enter covenant with us if we freely choose the same with God.

Another aspect of the burden of pluralism is that in our efforts to recognize and celebrate our diversity we are hard pressed to define and demonstrate our unity. Covenant calls us beyond independence. The significance of the call is that to which we are called. It is to go as a people into the center of our faith, the mystery of the union of grace where all things are one in the Christ Spirit of the gracious One whom we name God. This is a significant reason for the inclusive-evangelistic church to attend to its spiritual renewal. It is our religious essence that empowers us to serve. Without religious experience and a common language with which to speak of it we cannot covenant for unity, only diversity. In such a church pluralism is not only a burden, but also a curse because we will not be able to define ourselves to one another or to the world. Definition empowers. Lack of definition vitiates. The inclusive church has been wishy-washy primarily because it has not entered into and defined its religious essence.

Three Doors to the One Center

The covenanted community that values diversity understands that there are various ways to find one's way to the center where the mystery of God's grace finds us, ways other than the Christian way and ways within the Christian community, i.e., church. Within the churches I serve, three doors and subsequent ways to the center present themselves to me regularly: the spiritual door, the justice door, and the door of caring community. Each door is a way to enter the life of the people of God, but no one way is sufficient to sustain the life of the whole church. Each is needed for the benefit of the others. Those who enter through these doors follow the paths before them shaped by the door they entered. As they proceed on their journey of faith in the life of the church they will meet people who entered by other doors. If they are able to recognize their interdependence for the life of the whole church they will come nearer the essence of the God who calls them to the center. If they cannot value ways other than their own they deny the diversity in which the gospel is manifest, and their journey stops there until such time as interdependence is recognized.

To explore in more detail the nature of the three doors and their paths to the center we begin with the call of God, which initiates the journeys. God always calls in love. Various ones, hearing the call, will respond in various ways and enter by one of the three doors.

The Spiritual Door

Those who respond with a self-conscious pursuit of God undertake a self-proclaimed spiritual journey and enter by the spiritual door. Perhaps they recognize that the word comes from the midst of mystery. These pilgrims know more clearly than the others that it is God whom they seek. The religious experience found is union. The insight to be found is the unity of all creation. An active response to the call they hear is praise. Receptive response is quietness. What is received in the waiting/seeking is the revelation of God's grace, which when followed leads to the center of reality where the essence of God is profoundly experienced. The gifts to the pilgrims that flow from the revelation of grace are faith in God, a foundation of hope, and a deep reverence for the Creator and all creation. Among the insights that flow from the revelation is the understanding of the power of light and darkness. The power of darkness is in fear. The power of light is in love.

The Justice Door

The pilgrims who enter through the door of justice hear the call of God in love for the suffering people of the world. The call is to cherish and defend those who are abandoned, victimized, oppressed. The words of Jesus, "Inasmuch as you have ministered or not ministered unto the suffering ones you have or have not ministered to me" (Matt. 25:31–46), ring with clarity and power in the ears of this seeker. The religious experience found in this call is humility. The insight given is the worth and dignity of all people. Active response to the call is standing with the oppressed as together you defend them against individuals, principalities, and powers that use and/or abuse them. The receptive response is seeing with clear sight one's own and all others' complication in the evil, which diminishes and destroys us all when any one is diminished and/or destroyed. What is received in the seeing is the revelation of truth that, when followed, leads to the center.

Gifts that flow from the revelation are the knowledge that God is just, that there is hope in history, a love for neighbors, and faith in Jesus, the man for others. The insights that flow from the revelation having to do with the power of darkness and light show darkness's power in imperial structures and priorities, light's power resident in those who suffer.

The Caring Community Door

The pilgrims who pursue caring community hear the call of God's love as it is given and received in loving relationships. The call is for care givers and receivers within and beyond the community of faith. The religious experience found is belonging, being part of the Body of Christ and no longer a stranger or sojourner. Among the insights given is that vulnerability is a gift that opens persons one to the other in compassion and mutual support. These pilgrims' active response to finding caring community is caring in turn. Their receptive response is openness. What is received is intimacy with God and beloved friends. Gifts that flow from the revelation of the intimacy of God are love of self, faith in the Holy Spirit, and undying hope for loving relationship for all people. Insights regarding the power of darkness and light see darkness's power expressed in loneliness and the power of light in compassion.

There are gifts of the Spirit for the building up of the people of God, the community of faith, given to those who enter the various doors. As the center of the mystery of God's grace is approached, all pilgrims have their gifts to offer the others. But each must recognize that those who enter through different doors bring gifts for all. The gifts can be offered but not given. The initiative for receiving these gifts rests with each to whom the gifts are offered. If pride in one's call blinds one to the validity of the calls of the others, then that one's call atrophies into sterility and inhibits the life of the church rather than encourages it.

The call to spiritual life becomes ingrown and pietistic, self-righteous and narrow in its dogmatism and isolation if it is not corrected with the insights of the pilgrims who entered through the doors of justice and caring community. They know that God is not only found in the mystery of the spirit but also in the mystery found in relationships with real people.

The pilgrims called to justice can also become self-righteous and narrow, bitter and judgmental, soon identifying their cause as God's call rather than God's call as their cause. This happens when pride blinds them to both the need for humility and the praise of God, who is found in the worshipping community, in the mystery of the spiritual inquiry and the Spirit's response, as well as in relationship with those who are the outcasts of society. Similarly these pilgrims need to know of their need for, as well as the value to others of, mutual support and affection among believers.

The pilgrims called to caring community will come to value security above all else if they see only the care of the vulnerable within their faith community as the purpose of church life. The cry from the justice pilgrim to open doors to the afflicted on their doorsteps is a threat. The call from the seeker after the Spirit who dwells in the center of mystery is tolerated but discounted as ephemeral and too abstract to be of earthly good. The vital resources of prayer and worship are discounted. Institutional maintenance becomes mission, and controversy is not allowed in a healthy church. Thus the gift of difference is abandoned as troublesome, even dangerous. Any suggestion of one's culpability in the suffering of the world will be seen as intrusive and unfair because, as I have heard church members say, "Charity begins at home and I'm doing my part."

In the congregations I have served it is clear that among those called to the door of caring community there are some who are gifted for the task of institutional maintenance. These people possess management skills and/or interest in and abilities to oversee and participate in the care and maintenance of the facilities. Theirs is a genuine call to ministry, constructive as long as they recognize the validity and need for those called to serve God's purposes in ways represented by the other doors. They are subject to the seduction of seeing security as the purpose of good ministry, statistics as the measure of success, and the perpetuation of the institution as an end in itself. As they are open to the gifts others bring from their respective callings they understand the breadth of the mission to which the church is called. Their labors are then defined in terms of serving the overall mission of Christ's church through the maintenance of the institution rather than the institution as an end in itself. Again the Christ Spirit unites and makes a coordinated whole of our separate parts.

When those entering different doors can recognize, honor, and celebrate the gifts of the diversity of their pluralistic congregation, then each is blessed with balance and the gifts of Spirit, servanthood, and intimacy. The key to honoring the gifts of diversity and variety in God's calling is the experience of the grace of God found in the center of reality. The pilgrim seeking faithfulness in spiritual life is more clearly focused upon the object of this faith experience, but all pilgrims encounter the truth of God's love in Christ on their way. It is in this Christ Spirit that things are made new, brokenness is made whole, separateness knit together. The development of the God-centered world view of Christian life as opposed to the self-centered world view of secular life redefines power, success, security, status, and meaning in receptive, vulnerable, intimate, serving terms. This new view of the world is the key to the integration of diversity into unity and the mutual empowerment for God's purposes of all pilgrims by the gifts of each pilgrim.

In churches I have served, we work to gain understanding that each of us in the congregation is called to ministry, called by God to be who we are for God's purposes in the church and the world. I play fast and loose with metaphors and transform the three doors through which pilgrims enter the community of faith to the three pillars that support the ministry of the whole congregation. In this analogy the ministry of each and all of us is supported by the pillars of spiritual seekers, justice servers, and caring community enablers. If one of the pillars is not in place, the ministry of all suffers significantly. The structure tips and falls, becoming far less than it would be if all three were in place. Thus pictured, their interdependence is visually recognized. In this time in the life of our inclusive churches the spiritual pillar is the primary pillar, because if we are not a religious community, then we are not the church. At other times in our history one of the other pillars will need primary emphasis. But each is always needed for the health of the ministries to which we are called as individuals and for the shared ministry to which we are called as a community of faith.

CHAPTER 6

Two Parts of the Whole:
The Rational and the Intuitive

The World is too much with us; late and soon,
Getting and spending, we lay waste our powers,
Little we see in Nature that is ours;
We have given our hearts away, a sordid boon!
The Sea that bears her bosom to the moon;
The winds that will be howling at all hours,
And that are up-gathered now like sleeping flowers;
For this, for everything we are out of tune;
It moves us not.—Great God! I'd rather be
A Pagan suckled in a creed outworn;—
So might I, standing on this pleasant lea,
Have glimpses that would make me less forlorn;
Have sight of Proteus rising from the sea;
Or hear old Triton blow his wreathed horn.

—William Wordsworth
"The World is Too Much With Us"[1]

A rational approach to matters of the spirit has led to widespread claims of infallibility, exclusive righteousness, mechanical interpretations of religious experience, empty dogma, and ritual that results in conformity. On the other hand, spiritual intoxication without rational balance leads the individual into isolation; into experience as an end in itself; into fanaticism with its loss of direction and its redoubled effort; into addiction.

Can we in the inclusive church be open-minded and committed, open-spirited and faithful? We can and we must. The source of the unity that will reconcile the diversity and contradictions within and between us resides in the mystery of the grace of the One God.

The radical monotheism of the Hebrew tradition gives us direction for understanding the unity found in God. Twentieth-century rationality is apt to interpret monotheism only as an option of objective choice, an either/or preference between believing in one God, several Gods, or no God. We tend to overlook the mystical implications of monotheism, assuming it meant what it thought but not what it felt. Monotheism does not speak only of the God of Israel being the God of all. It also reflects the experience of the nature of God in whom all things have unity and, paradoxically, because all truth is composed of opposites, through whom all things have unique identity.

Recent research and theory having to do with the functions of the right and left hemispheres of the human brain provide a model of the unity the inclusive church can champion. The thinking of Robert Ornstein, in particular, has been helpful in formulating a model for understanding the polarity of which I speak and the possibility of integration.

Brain Hemispheres: A Model For the Church

In Ornstein's fascinating book, *The Psychology of Consciousness*, he presents recent discoveries of the contrasting and complementary function of the right and left hemispheres of the brain. He refers to two major modes of consciousness: the analytic and the holistic. He writes,

> [These major modes of consciousness] are complementary; both have their functions. Another way to convey the dichotomy is to point to the difference between the "rational" and the "intuitive" sides of man. In our intellectual history, we have separated these two modes of knowing into separate areas of specialization, into Science and Religion, for example.[2]

Both the structure and the function of these two "half-brains" in some part underlie the two modes of consciousness that simultaneously coexist within each one of us.

In summary of Ornstein and the literature telling of the functions of the left and right hemisphere, although both hemispheres share abilities for many functions in most people, each side specializes. The left hemisphere is most often the center of rational, analytic, sequential thought, the center for verbal and mathematical thinking, for example, and the memory of names. The right hemisphere is most often the center of intuitive, holistic thought. Orientation in multidimensional rather than sequential experiences is specialized here. Abstract thought, artistic expression, mystical experience, and recognition of faces would seem to originate in the right hemisphere.

Interestingly, as the data supporting the understanding of the various functions of the right and left hemispheres began to accumulate, the hemispheres were called the "major" and the "minor" hemispheres. Recognizing that it is scientific research processes gathering the data, it is not hard to guess that the rational or left hemisphere would be called major. Of course, both are major. Beethoven, Georgia O'Keeffe, Picasso, Mother Teresa, or Jesus would have been less than significant persons if they had lost the functioning of their right hemisphere. But the thrust of this discussion is not to advocate the intuitive over the rational, but to affirm the necessity of each for the continued participation of humanity in the creation. Unfortunately, the history of western culture suggests alternating periods of domination of one mode of thought over the other rather than a unity that values and integrates the insights of both.

Native Americans: An Intuitive Cultural Model

A classic conflict of the rational and the intuitive modes of thought and cultural styles was acted out in the settling of the western United States during the latter third of the nineteenth century. What historians call the Indian Wars was the conflict that defeated the more passive and intuitively oriented cultures of the North American Indians. This does not mean that the Native Americans were pacifists. They were fighting among themselves long before Europeans set foot on their land. This does not alter the fact that, by and large, the relationship of the American Indians to their tribe, their land, and the Great Spirit demonstrated greater awe and respect for the interrelationship of all things, for wholeness than was to be found in the aggressive and ambitious culture that took their place on most of the land.

The fruits of the rational mind, technology and its hardware, coupled with a myopic faith that interpreted God as European and saw salvation as the gift that could be found only in European interpretations of divine will, armed the greed of western expansion across North America. The more intuitive cultures of the American Indians, although fiercely loyal to tribe, allowed the existence of other religious truth than their own in their world view, culture *vs.* creation. The Indian willingness to consider coexistence, a decision influenced by their environment, life-style and belief systems, provided a foothold for European presence that led to inevitable conflicts and their ultimate subjugation—a way of life past. What is slowly being learned now, however, is that the essential aspects of the way of life that sprang from American Indian intuitive genius are needed in the culture that supplanted it if the supplanting culture is to adjust and continue. This is in no way more clearly seen than in the crisis of environment and ecology.[3]

In search of access to the American Indian religious way and perspective on their method of mystical experience and inquiry it was my privilege to visit with Ellis Chips and his family on the Lakota Sioux reservation in Wambly, South Dakota, in the winter of 1976–77. I went with a friend and fellow Christian minister, Terry Gibson, to meet and learn from Mr. Chips. He had been recommended to us as a medicine man of the tribe and the head of a family with a tradition of medicine people. We were hoping that personal contact in the context of Ellis Chips's family and home would expand our understanding of the way of Sioux Indian religion.

Among our findings, we learned that there is one sacred object in the worship practice of the Chips family: the sacred pipe. It is a pipe passed on to Ellis from his father, also a medicine man, who received it in turn from his father who was medicine man to the great Sioux warrior and leader, Crazy Horse. We were told that it was Ellis's grandfather who provided Crazy Horse with a power stone that he wore to protect himself from the bullets of the white American soldiers he was fighting.

Ellis also told us that it was his grandfather who took the body of Crazy Horse and buried it in the badlands so that the white men could never find it. Pictures of the grandfather and father hang on the wall of the Chips home as if to bear witness to the central prayer of his people, "To pray for generations to come and for one to right the wrong," which he chants during the daily prayer service.

The Prayer of the Sacred Pipe is chanted while the pipe is lit and passed around the circle of communicants. It translates into English as follows:

> Grandfather, Great Spirit I shall not consider myself
>   above you.
> Now shall I consider myself equal to you.
> Under the heavens you have created all the fowls of
>   the air,
> And all the four-legged creatures.
> You have also created all the animals living under the
>   ground.
> You have created all the animals living in the water
>   to the depths of the waters.
> And many different kinds of trees you have created,
> Along with different kinds of plants and herbs,
> And many different kinds of weeds and grass.
> And all the different kinds of animals you have
>   created eat to survive the many different kinds
>   of weeds, grass, and the plants.
> We Indians survive on the land, the fruit of the
>   trees; when sick we eat and use the herbs.
> To each of the four directions of the wind and to the
>   heavens and on the earth, you have created to
>   seat spirits to watch over Mother Earth and you
>   have instored powers in these spirits to hear
>   our every prayer.
> This sacred pipe was brought to the Indian people and
>   with these two rulings: to pray for generations
>   to come and for one to right the wrong.
> In all this universe I ask the leaders of the animal
>   kingdom, to you who have power, pray for us to
> God through the sacred pipe, for I ask for every good
>   thing and for generation after generation to
>   come.

Ellis believes that human beings cannot pray directly to God because they are not pure enough to warrant direct access. It is to the animals who lead natural lives, who do no other than their

God-given instincts direct, that "the power," i.e., direct access to the great Spirit, belongs.

Ellis is not a "wichasha wakon," or holy man. He has no power of his own. His son Godfrey, reported to have power, is a wichasha wakon. Ellis has responsibility for the sacred pipe and acts as liturgist in the prayer service. Ellis can hear the spirits but cannot interpret them. He does not understand them. Godfrey hears and understands the spirits.

Godfrey does not possess the power of the leaders of the animal kingdom to act as messengers of Indian prayers, but he does receive messages. The messages tell him of future events and instruct him in healing, which he performs either with the patient present or absent. Any act of healing or telling of the future is preceded by patient and detailed preparation involving purification and the prayers of the pipe. The prayer of the pipe is always the same prayer. The request or petitions of the various persons in the prayer service are "under the pipe." They are not seen as prayers to the Great Spirit but as requests of the mediating spirits. Harmony with the Great Spirit is necessary, however, if requests are to be granted.

Reincarnation is a part of the Sioux religion in Ellis Chips's interpretation. If an individual lived a good life, he or she will quickly be born into another body. If he or she lived an exceptionally good life, his or her spirit will go to dwell with the Great Spirit. If one leads a bad life, he or she will be left in a ghost form on earth to observe and learn for a period of time, the longer period for the worst offenders against the law of perpetuating the generations and righting wrongs.[4]

Another item of interest regards the Chips's oldest son, Charles. Charles was preparing to take over the administration of the sacred pipe and went through the initiation procedures in the summer of 1977. He told us that he had three requests of the spirits that will be granted if he leads a good life. He emphasized patience in waiting for the granting of the requests but expressed no doubt that they would be forthcoming. His requests were for the ability to tell the future, to heal, and to remake the past. I was particularly interested in the last request. He was glad to explain it but had some difficulty doing so. I then offered an interpretation of what he was saying in my words. "Do you mean that you want to be able to understand the past and explain it to others so that they will see it in new ways?" He agreed that that was what he meant. I was sure that I had not caught all of what he hoped to say, but we silently agreed that that was probably as much as I could understand.

The Indian understanding of time, not fully in tune with our sequential approach, was reflected in two ways. One was the way Ellis Chips told his stories. They came to us as verbal collage rather than spun tales. Sequence of events was not nearly as important as the nature of events. He had a keen sense of humor and laughed easily at his own jokes, having on occasion to point out to me the discontinuity that made the joke. He was exceptionally quick to see the humor we offered in return and laughed heartily with us. His nonsequential approach was not due to an inability to see contrast or understand order. It suggested an artist painting a picture, working on one part for awhile, leaving it to work on another, and then returning to work more on what he had first begun.

The other nonsequential understanding of time was in the ready acceptance of the abilities to look into the future and reach into the past. Although we were not able to follow these ideas up in our conversation, they were clearly there. It is obvious, however, that if one believes it is possible to tell the future and reach into the past, then he or she does not see time flowing by as a river into which one cannot step twice. Here is a case where so-called primitive religions seem in touch with concepts of time that our leading physicists are just comprehending.

Is the Church Two-Brained?

What does this brief look into Sioux religion have to do with the Christian church? What we are considering is a paradigm of our cultural conditioning found in the discussion about the two hemispheres of the brain and their functions, intuitive and rational. The mind is capable of far more than we generally seem able to exercise.

Truth, handicapped by an either/or mentality, is thought of as pure, without contradiction. Thus, many have claimed their perception of one pole of reality to be all of reality. This reflects the dependence in Western thought upon the rational mode of understanding, for it is this way of understanding that organizes ideas sequentially and defines events in cause and effect, either/or categories. The ways of American Indian religion, representing an intuitive valuing world view, are alive and in touch with spirits of the earth and animals, power visions from the Great Spirit and ceremonies of preparation and patience that open their people to harmonious relationships with one another, with nature and her Creator Mystery.

What one culture has seen as realities has been scoffed at as superstition by another. Though psychic and mystical experience has been spoken of throughout the history of western civilization, a dependence upon the rational mode of thought from classical thought, reaffirmed in the Enlightenment, shapes our contemporary materialistic world view and has had great influence upon our religious perceptions and definitions. Many Christians, for example, call for literal interpretations of the Bible, which is a rational demand upon an intuitive literature. Salvation is defined in either/or terms with clear definition given to the saved and the damned. Using imagination to seek truth beyond fact is little understood and minimally valued. The unifying spirit of God that makes all things one, in which categories of the damned and the saved become greatly blurred by grace, is diminished by a segregating spirit that seems to need to define self in and others out. All of this definition and separation is logical, linear, mechanical—in other words, dominated by rational thought.

Both sides of the cerebral cortex are God-given and necessary for the continuation of the creation if human beings are to be a part of it. Yes, this opens us up to much that cannot be understood or proven by acceptable scientific processes. Yes, we let in the mystics, the healers, the visionaries, the prophets. We risk losing control. The authority of the rational does bring order but at the price of the loss of soul, unless room is made for the intuitive as full partner in perception and reality definition. Our rational theologies and our restricting orthodoxies must interact with the intuitive experience of all believers.

Let in the mystics, the healers, the visionaries, the prophets? Yes! We need to rediscover how to open to the spirit and let it blow through us with fresh word—but not as an end in itself. We must learn to exercise the right hemisphere in the life of the church but not at the expense of abandoning the left, despite the tension in the task.

Ornstein tells how the study of the right and left hemisphere was greatly enhanced by an operation designed to aid epileptics.

It severed the corpus callosum, stopping the interchange of information between the two sides. What resulted was "two-brained" persons. An individual could see mathematical data with his or her left eye but could not get the information to the left hemisphere to articulate it. Similarly, pictures that invoked feelings were shown to the right eye but not to the left. There was no way for the individual with the severed brain to get the explanation for the feelings to the right hemisphere. Ornstein writes of the experiment,

> emotion-laden information was given to the right hemisphere while the verbal hemisphere remained unaware of it. A photograph of a nude woman was shown to the right hemisphere of a patient in the course of a series of otherwise dull laboratory tests. At first, the woman viewing the nude on the screen said that she saw nothing, then immediately flushed, alternately squirmed, smiled, and looked uncomfortable and confused. But her "conscious" or verbal half was still unaware of what had caused the emotional turmoil which was occurring in her body. Her words reflected that the emotional reaction had been "unconscious," unavailable to her language apparatus. To paraphrase her, "What a funny machine you have there, [doctor]."[5]

Is this not a fair metaphor for the church that has not learned how to integrate its intellectual and its feeling responses, its rational and its intuitive, its institutional and its spontaneous, its social witness with its inner life? What is being suggested is that a healthy individual and a healthy church must be open to and integrate spiritual nature and calling with active nature and calling. The one centers in the intuitive and the other in the rational. They need one another so that the work of the unit be effective and open, seeking to do the will of the God of Jesus Christ and our God who speaks to us in the still small voice and through the whirlwind.

Using analogy, Ornstein describes persons attuned to the intuitive as being people of the night who stay indoors during the day. They are observers of the stars, make notations of their movement, and write poems of their influence. Others are day people and, try as they may, they cannot see the subtle lights in the heavens the poets of the night describe. Their conclusion: stars exist only in the minds of night people. Following this he writes, meditation is a technique for tuning down the brilliance of the day, so that ever-present and subtle sources of energy can be perceived within. It constitutes a deliberate attempt to separate oneself for a short period from the flow of daily life, and to "turn off" the active mode of normal consciousness in order to enter the complementary mode of "darkness" and receptivity.[6]

The intuitive, the visions and dreams, the still small voice is always speaking. The volume of the active mode is turned so high in our normal lives that we have few ways to hear the intuitive, except during occasional pauses such as those caused when tragedy stops us cold or beauty breaks through with an impact that cannot be denied. We have all heard the still voice, the silent music. It echoes in our dreams and frustrates our successes in the active world. God is in the stillness speaking, calling, cajoling, shaping, caring. It is to our benefit and to the benefit of the world that we hear.

Spiritual Sight

Pierre Teilhard de Chardin speaks of the coexistence of the Without and the Within of things.

> It is impossible to deny that, deep within ourselves an "interior" appears at the heart of beings, as it were seen through a rent. This is enough to ensure that, in one degree or another, this "interior" should obtrude itself as existing everywhere in nature from all time. Since the stuff of the universe has an inner aspect at one point of itself, there is necessarily a *double aspect* to its structure, that is to say in every region of space and time . . . *co-extensive with their Without, there is a Within to things.*[7]

Martin Buber speaks of the same phenomenon as he directs us to value the "thou" aspects of all beings, to see deeper than their utility into their essence. When the essence is seen it is recognized to be of the essence of the divine "Thou"; thus it is with the Within of things, using Teilhard de Chardin's word.

Spiritual sight, to truly see another and to see God, is the beginning of becoming what the Sioux call "a human being"; what

Jesus calls "a good and faithful servant"; what we would call "being a Christian." Teilhard de Chardin encourages our development of another dimension of spiritual sight, creation itself:

> By means of all created things, without exception, the divine assails us, penetrates us, molds us. We imagine it as distant and inaccessible, whereas we live steeped in its burning layers . . .
>
> God reveals Himself everywhere, beneath our groping efforts, as universal milieu . . . [8]

God is the milieu and God is in the particulars that exist within the milieu. God is not limited to one thing but is present there nonetheless. Spiritual sight reveals God in and around all things.

Spiritual sight is not an end, but a means of perceiving beauty, meaning, and purpose, i.e., meeting God. With developed sight into the mystery of being we can "see" God. This is the ultimate revelation immanently available, as Teilhard de Chardin tells us, all around us, "steeped in burning layers." Seeing the beauty, we not only rejoice in it, but we seem to have no choice but to love it as well. From that love springs the energy to affirm and defend the dignity and beauty recognized. From that love springs our mandate to do justice.

We all use spiritual, intuitive sight in some degree but seldom realize that it is religious experience. Some thrill at the sight of a bird, others when hearing certain music; many know and want to continue knowing the deep satisfaction of being loved. Spiritual experience may be in nature or art. Perhaps you find it in literature or the feel of clay taking shape in your hands. It could be an active dream life or vivid imagination. You may be moved by cathedrals and stained glass or perhaps by a plain white church with clear windows. You may sense eternity in a flower or hear a voice in the wind that calls you to greater things. The voices that speak to our intuitive ears are active, albeit softly, and determined. We are restless until we find rest with God, which is our completion, our holiness. The many voices of creation speak through that inner ear; those many spectral visions beat upon our heavy-lidded inner eyes. These are the perceptions to be acknowledged and expanded. They open upon an understanding that mystics through the ages and across the cultures bear witness to. They reveal God.

Developing Your Spiritual Life

The first thing to be said about developing the life of your spirit is that another's experience cannot be given or forced upon you. You must choose to pursue it. There must be a conscious decision to look and listen in order to see what can be seen and heard from a realm of reality that cannot be proven to exist. There is an objective test for reality in the material world view that cannot be made of the religious world view. Thus many will consider intuited reality improbable and imagined perceptions foolish. Such is a risk one takes if one chooses to develop understanding of the broader reality that our whole brain can comprehend.

Spiritual truth cannot be proven to you. You must recognize your need and follow your inclinations into the realm of faith that opens on the mystery of being. The testimony of men and women across the centuries and across cultures is that the life of the spirit is real and, when discovered and developed, indispensable to expanded existence, wholeness, holiness of persons and cultures. You will recognize realities unfolding that have been hinted at in your awareness. It is a journey worth taking, but you must choose to take it by saying yes to the One who stands outside the door of your soul and knocks to be let in.

Secondly, let me warn against certainty. The life of the spirit does not offer certainty. It is not the realm of creed or dogma, doctrine or orthodoxy. These may be guides for you, noble efforts to articulate past journeys of the soul and tell of what was found. You may be able to own those statements as reflections of truth you too have or hope to find, but they are not the Truth—only reflections of it. The Truth of the spirit is experienced in dimensions that frustrate language to replicate. Although those who have experienced the mystery of life, of God, of being know for certain that they have been touched, they cannot be certain of all that was involved in the experience. However, they are able to point in the direction from which they have come and tell of the experience and the direction in which it leads.

Authority Is at Issue

What is the authority for your spiritual experience? How do you know that what you believe is true? Who tells you? How can it be verified? Is the authority outside or within you? If your friend or minister or bishop says something you don't agree with about religion or ethics, what is the basis of your contradiction? What right do you have to disagree? Do you quote scripture to justify your position? Do you appeal to revelation, spiritual enlightenment?

Certainly there are others who know more than we about most everything. Is intellect the criterion for authority? Because someone has read more books, is he or she wise? Does your experience count? Do your insights have validity? What about your feelings? Do they carry any weight on the scale of decision-making to which you look for direction?

My perspective is that there is authority within you that is of God. It is what I believe Jesus had in mind when he said, "Seek first [God's] Realm and righteousness, and all these things will be yours as well" (Matt. 6:33). And where is the realm of God? It is coming and it is with us (Matt. 10:7, 12:28). God's realm is not all found within, but it is within us, each of us. Jesus directs us into our own spiritual experience, into our intuitive perceptions. And there is more—coming not by our action, but by God's.

We can search within and find something of God's will, God's direction. That is what the realm of God is: the area of divine influence. It is a force field constantly pulling at us, yet one we must choose to recognize in order to become increasingly aware of the attraction and the harmony of the patterns it establishes. Like iron shavings arranged by the force field of a magnet, our lives can become harmonious with God's will as we receive and open ourselves to it.

The knowledge that God's realm is found within us as well as from beyond encourages us to enter the life of our own spirit. Our task is the discovery and development of our spiritual capacities and opening to God's influence. We have the freedom to resist, even to refuse the opportunity. God will not give up on us, however; nor will God leave the establishment of ultimate purposes up to us. God is the authority and God's will is supreme, but we are invited to be consciously involved in the process.

In a unique way, a way that reflects grace in its design, we are authority for the recognition of the presence of God's reign within and about us. Describing the truth we know is finally a faith statement for which we each are individually responsible, but our truth is not all of Truth, and we are not alone in our perceptions nor without help to understand further dimensions. Accompanying and available to us are the stories of our faith and tradition, voices of seekers and finders over the generations that speak from our Bible, Jesus Christ above all. The Holy Spirit brings those voices to life and correlates their truth to ours. And, in that Christianity is a faith of a people, not just persons, we have the gift of our faith community to encourage our seeking, challenge and confirm our finding. In that community there are not only those with whom we presently worship but also the cloud of witnesses that surround us, the many generous souls past and present in the Christian tradition who offer their views and stories as help for our consideration. Then there are other traditions and seekers within the Christian faith and other faith traditions that have perspectives on Truth that is light for our seeing. But the initial and final authority for us in the verification of Truth is our own intuitive knowing. Informed by life and love in all its incarnational forms, for Christians by Jesus above all, by the church as the body of Christ, we nonetheless must say yes based on a knowing beyond reason. The "yes" is our moment of conversion.

A Bridge to Religious Understanding and Practice

The bridge of faith leads from the dominant world view of our time to the God-centered world view of our biblical tradition, crossing over a torrent of contradiction and confusion. The dominant world view of western culture is grounded in faith in the ability of the human mind, using its skills of logic and rationality, to define and confirm what is real. It is a world view with decided preferences for individualism and control whereas the God-centered world view has decided preferences for interdependent relationships and admitted vulnerability. Poetry, myth, metaphor, and paradox, although the essential language of religions, are interesting but too murky to be the stuff of reality for a world view built upon human rationality.

Rationality plays significant roles in all aspects of human life and has an essential part to play in religious understanding and communication. It helps categorize and test the accounts of the exploration of mystery even though it cannot enter a relationship with the sacred found in mystery. Many of us have been led to the edge of mystery by rationality and have found mystery in the wonders of order and system in creation discovered and defined by rational inquiry. But the experience of the sacred that encounters us in mystery is beyond rationality's reach. Rationality points; imagination enters.

Religious language and literature, the product of creativity given expression in the linear-rational process of words, always point beyond themselves to the divine initiator who cannot be defined. They realize that the truth of which they speak is found in experience but cannot be captured for storage in objective mental containers. Poetry and great literature can regenerate experiences of the sacred and thus act as reminders and encouragers of sacred experience. They can even lead us beyond truths of the Spirit previously understood to new places of experience and understanding, but it is precisely because they engage our imaginations to move beyond objective categories and definitions that new vistas are found. God is neither a specimen for our intellectual museums nor an object to be defined in dogma or creed. Creeds have their place as testimony of religious experiences of times recently or long ago past. They are also invitations to a present experience and knowing of the reality and truth for which they were created to bear witness. They point and invite. They do not encapsulate the truth. Creeds are religious art forms.

If we choose to recognize and follow the presence and truth of God's grace we will need to develop capacities of spiritual perception and experience that many of us have been taught to ignore or deny. The earlier discussion of right and left hemisphere abilities is once more a model for the task. The corpus callosum is the bridge between the two hemispheres. We need to find bridges to connect our secular and religious worlds. We need a bridge because the traffic has to be two-way. We need a connection that allows legitimacy and mutual edification of our rational and intuitive experience. Building the bridge is the faith development work most appropriately and effectively done within and with one's church as it teaches and encourages the individual and community spiritual practices of contemplation.

The bridge is essentially the faith to believe that there is more than objective reality, and that the meaning of life is found in truth revealed in mystery, the subjective experience of relationships with God, neighbor, and self. Another word for such faith is imagination. Crossing the bridge to religious understanding and practice is accomplished by a willingness to develop and explore what one's imagination does with rational and intuitive perceptions of truth found in relationships with God, self, and others.

The bridge of faith moves us from our present knowledge of God into mystery where greater knowledge is found. It begins with what spiritual truth we know and leads us to deeper understanding. The conversion from a view of the world centered in our ability to define and control to a God-centered world happens along this way. If the conversion has happened previously, the way leads to deeper understanding. The knowledge, the understanding of God of which I speak comes as the consequence of relationship with God who is met in the mystery of grace.

CHAPTER 7

Finding God in the Mystery: An Individual and Community Experience

> For it is the God who said, "Let light shine out of darkness," who has shone in our hearts to give the light of the knowledge of the glory of God in the face of Christ.
>
> 2 Cor. 4:6

A contemporary God-centered world view does not abandon rational perception and understands the need for human beings to exert some degree of control over their lives. In large measure any accountability that we have to God assumes and affirms our rational ability to discriminate between options and to take responsibility for our behavior. The major difference in the paths of the dominant world view and the God-centered world view is not that one embraces and the other abandons rationality. Instead, it is the point of how ultimate reality is approached and perceived. A God-centered world view does well to begin with imagination, depending upon intuition, listening, receptivity, and willingness to give up control to God, who is the ultimate reality. God is experienced in mystery more than fact, more accurately given expression in legend and myth than dogma or written definition. A God-centered world view values mystery and the human faculties that address, experience, and explore it. Rationality depends upon its own initiative. The experience of God depends upon God's initiative.

The bridge of imagination exists at the beginning of the spiritual journey of western women and men to help them across the strong current of contradiction and confusion between rational and mystical knowing. I am reminded of a conversation my son, then five, and I had when he asked, "Do we believe that God made the world?"

"Yes Jay, that is what we believe."

"Well, if God made the world, who made God?"

"We believe that God always was."

After a pause to consider my faith statement Jay responded, "I can't find that in my mind."

After a further pause I responded, "I can't find it in my mind either, Jay. Some things about God are bigger than our minds can hold. They can only be held by belief. Can you imagine that?"

The bridge of imagination is there on the path because the gifts of rational perception are not to be abandoned but rather to be gone beyond. The bridge metaphor is strained at this point because there is a continual crossing back and forth in our minds as we perceive and process information about reality, ultimate and penultimate. The corpus callosum connecting the right and left hemispheres of the brain is a better metaphor for this aspect of religious thinking, which we will cover later. For now let the bridge stand, if you will, representing a necessary movement from one faith system about how ultimate reality is perceived to another.

Grace at the Center of the Mystery

Our churches need to provide ways for members and other seekers who come to the doors to learn of the existence of the God-centered world view of our Bible and its difference from the world view of our culture. We need to develop ways to aid one another to improve the abilities we all possess to experience, trust, and explore the mystery within which God is revealed, a mystery that pervades and undergirds all reality. The essence of God, the God of Jesus Christ and our God, dwells in this mystery that, when revealed, is known to many as grace. It is a radiant paradoxical grace born of the intercourse of intimacy and transcendence, revealed as gift through our imagination. The intimacy is one of tender mercy and caressing affection. The transcendence is so expansive, brutal, and radiant as to be blinding in its appearance and obliterating in its presence. Grace, the offspring, is best understood in vulnerability and servanthood, more the child of intimacy than transcendence, yet clearly parented by both.

A Shadow Aspect of the Mystical Experience

For various reasons many in our inclusive Protestant tradition have shied away from, even deprecated the worth and influence of mysticism in Christianity. Chief among the criticisms is that the mystical vision is essentially a personal experience beyond confirmation or coordination, tending to a blindness to the God of history and community, with the individual in authority. It is argued that the authority of the tradition, of the faith as continued in the church, is eroded by the relativistic aspects of individualism in religious experience. Accountability to the truth that has been revealed and refined over the ages is diminished or lost.

This is not just a defensive protest of male-dominated hierarchies fearing the loss of control to passion and imagination but a legitimate concern, calling attention to the shadowy side of ecstatic experience, the individualization of truth. Although the ultimate authority for truth is within you and the mystical experience can be a revelation of the deepest truth of God and the creation available to us, it is a personal experience, subject to prideful claims and myopic denials of the perspectives of other individuals or faith systems. The mystical vision within the context of the Christian faith and community speaks of crucifixion and resurrection, of Good Fridays and Easters. Without the biblical tradition and the history of the faith community as well as one's contemporary community of faith, the aspects of the life of faith that involve loss as well as gain can too easily be ignored or denied. This is particularly so in the consumer culture of late twentieth-century America.

Many in our western world are choosing the private exploration of religious experience, outside traditional faith communities, as their preferred mode of spiritual inquiry. A study conducted by the Gallup Organization for the Princeton Religion Research Center found that when asked to respond to the statement, "An individual should arrive at his or her own religious beliefs independent of any church or synagogue," 80 percent said yes. Forty-eight percent strongly agreed, 32 percent moderately agreed, 8 percent were undecided, 8 percent moderately disagreed, and 4 percent strongly disagreed.[1] This 80 percent contains most of the people who are presently members of churches and synagogues, whose influence appears to be seen to inhibit if not obstruct one's spiritual quest. The radical individualism of our culture that Robert Bellah and colleagues so helpfully chronicle in *Habits of the Heart* is revealed here. Does this reflect a distrust of authority in institutional form? Perhaps it is a comment on the poverty of aid to be found in our churches for the spiritual journey. Whatever it is, it suggests that many people are trusting their ability to find religious truth without accountability to or support from a traditional faith community. This raises the question: can revelation based in ecstatic experience endure the struggles of life that continue beyond the mystical insight?

The early Christian communities were struggling with the dark side of ecstatic experience that fragmented the common faith and fractured community. They valued and encouraged spiritual experience but subjected it to accountability through the community. Gifts of the Spirit were tested, held up to a standard of loving relationships informed by the grace of God in Jesus Christ. Paul's first letter to the Corinthians acknowledges that speaking in tongues and other gifts of the spirit have their place but are secondary to the gift of grace, which is agape, the love of which he speaks in 1 Cor. 13. In 1 Thess. 5:19–21 we read of the need to test the individual experiences of the Spirit. "Do not quench the Spirit, do not despise prophesying, but test everything; hold fast what is good." In 2 Cor. 12 Paul chastises the Jewish Christians who went to Corinth after he had left for they defied his authority, claiming their own ecstatic experiences and works of wonder as superior to his. Paul affirms ecstatic experience, referring to his own mystical breakthrough on the road to Damascus, but ultimately, he says, the truth of God in Christ is proved in the power of weakness. The central message is in verse 9, which is God's response to Paul's pleas to free him of his "thorn in the flesh," his suffering that persisted in spite of his mystical experience. Paul says God's answer to his pleas as, "My grace is sufficient for you, for my power is made perfect in weakness."

The Benefit of Christian Community in the Quest for God

Bellah and friends tell of a woman named Sheila, who had been helped by psychotherapy to find and affirm herself. She was using that model of private introspection to continue her spiritual quest. Sheila chose the smorgasbord approach to spiritual development characteristic of the radical individualism of western culture. She picked and chose according to her tastes. When asked what faith she claimed as hers she paused a moment and then said "Sheilaism."[2]

It is the prospect of this self-centered consumer approach to faith that many leery of mysticism fear. It is a legitimate fear. Such faith in one's independent ability to discern and decide what is true is too often blind to the myopia of cultural conditioning. Again the lesson taught me by a friend on the outside of established culture is relevant. She not only taught me that those on the outside cannot get the attention of those who are inside until they hurt us, but that the reason we must be hurt is because we are blind to ways of seeing, experiencing, and knowing that are other than our own. Women know this of men. Ethnic minorities know it of the ethnic majority. Gays, lesbians, and bisexuals know it of heterosexuals. The poor know it of the affluent. Religious people know it of the secular majority. All of us know it in one way or another for we are all outside in some degree. Perhaps the pain of our exclusion is why so many of us, when we find ourselves on the inside, close our minds to outsiders.

Sheila searches in the dimness and light of her individual perspective for eternal truth, and she will find some aspects of it. God knocks on the door of every soul. What she finds may lead to a unity of her heart and mind, a unity of God and self. Our prayer will be that she does. But there is an aspect of God's Truth that cannot be found alone. How will she break out of her cultural isolation? How will she find the truth that only those outside of her own perspective have for her? How will she know that the truth she has found can be trusted even though her suffering does not end? The experience and resources of a community of faith—caring seekers and finders who have been through and continue in the struggle involved in believing in a God revealed in Jesus— would be of significant help to her in her search for God.

A vital and creative Christian faith is open to the mystical experience of God found in traditional and nontraditional forms, but it does not base its understanding on mystical revelation alone. In the inclusive church one is held accountable through community to the truth of Christian tradition found in scripture, to the wisdom gained throughout the history of the faith both within and beyond its denomination of choice, as well as beyond

Christianity. But if the church is to live and survive it will open to, be encouraging of and empowered by the experience of God known as the mystical experience. Moreover, it will support and encourage you in your spiritual journey.

Let us imagine Sheila joining not just any Christian church, but the ideal community of inclusive evangelical believers. It is not without its tension and misunderstanding, but it is committed to and trusting of God and one another. There would be accountability to the truth of the Christian faith tradition as it is explored and defined in her faith community. There would be the wealth of the stories of the faith journeys of the members of her covenanted community. Her individual journey of faith with its discoveries would form a part of that wisdom. She would not find it easy to be accountable to a God that the dominant culture does not serve or believe in. There would be pain involved. Her previous individualized spirituality would find the pain that comes as a consequence of individual and community imperfections difficult to endure. A major reason for individualized spiritual journeys is to find a purity of belief and devotion where compromises will not need to be made, where imperfections are either overcome or ignored. Confessed vulnerability marks this community's level of trust.

There would be pain because the mutual acceptance of this community affirms differences that are not all easy to live with. The mark of this faith community is its commitment to believe and live the honest and forgiving way of Jesus. Their faith allows the beginning of honesty about themselves and the secular aspects of their society that worships Mammon in search of safety, not the God of Jesus Christ.

This community affirms and calls out one another's gifts. She would find the affirmation of self that she cherished in therapy— the essence of the Christian gospel, the good news of grace. But it is much more than therapy can provide. She would find herself within community covenanted with God and friends in faith rooted in the tradition of Moses, the prophets, and Paul, faith in the grace of God given its fullest expression in the life, death, and resurrection of Jesus. In covenanted community she will have lost the appearance of independence for the experience of interdependence. It is a greater freedom than her belief in the value of independence could provide. The freedom found in faith in the grace of God of the Christian faith is not a freedom from others but freedom for God found in love and service with and for others.

If Sheila were to choose another Christian community than the ideal described, one that holds a high regard for the cultural idols of freedom as an end in itself, of numbers as the primary measurement of institutional success, of nostalgia as grace, of safety to be more blessed than vulnerability, of homogeneity as the essence of community, if she chooses a community of faith captured by the self-centered world view of our secular culture, then she will continue in her semidarkness with those culturally blinded ones with whom she has chosen to identify.

If Sheila chooses to search for God in any of the congregations that I know she will find some combination of the above models. The first mentioned is a Christian community that is in but not of the world. The second is the culture dependent pseudo-Christian community that is in and of the world. Not only do both models exist in our congregations, but some aspects of them also exist in each one of us in every congregation. Our hope is that we as individuals and communities of faith can confess our complex devotions and seek faithfully toward the pure hearts that Jesus encourages in the Sermon on the Mount. Our hope is not that we will reach that purity but that God's grace will be known to us and through us as we seek after faithfulness together.

Faithfulness: Following the Sight of God

Jesus says that those of pure heart will be blessed with the sight of God (Matt. 5:8). Søren Kierkegaard helps me to understand this beatitude when he says, "Purity of heart is to will one thing."[3] Hearing Jesus teach about the necessity of choosing whom we will serve between God and Mammon (Matt. 6:24), of the appropriate search for a stone rather than sand foundation for the home we would build (Matt. 7:24–27), of seeking first the reign of God's love in our life and letting all else fall into place (Matt. 6:33) leads us to seek purity of heart by willing to be faithful to God. That one thing we would will is faithfulness to God who is seen by the Christ light that shines in the mystery of loving relationships.

Being faithful in community means being faithful in relationships. Martin Buber was right when he said that there is no existence outside of relationship; we can choose to relate to others and the world without acknowledging the sacred in those with whom we relate. But the sacred is there nonetheless. The great Thou of existence is in each thou we find in relationships of mutuality, compassion, playfulness, and delight. When we miss the thou, the sacred in others, through ignorance or choice, we see objects existing for purposes of our definition, our manipulation. This vision leads to dreariness and death.[4] Being faithful in relationships means believing that the one or ones with whom we are relating are loved by God. Sometimes that is easier to see than at other times, but as the faith of Jesus says, whether we can see why or not, it is true.

Our call to faithfulness is to follow Jesus, the embodiment of God's mystical grace, through the fire storm of the secular materialistic individualism that is devouring our society. How can we do it? Paradox again raises its double-helix head. Although the individual search for the God of Christianity is most appropriately conducted in community, it finds its truth in uniquely individual moments of mystical experience. The experience of God, the One in whom all things are One, reveals the power of love: unmitigated, unmodified, blatant, skin-scorching, soul-searing, blast-furnace refining, melting, melding, world-stopping-and-beginning-again, down-on-your-knees, cover-your-face, tremble-in-your-vulnerability *power*. This fearsome power holds you tenderly in its loving and safe embrace. This power sends galaxies spinning into space and holds every other human being to its loving breast, gazing upon their faces with rapt awe and soul-binding affection, just the way that it holds you. This One, awesome to behold and compassionate beyond reason, loves each one and the whole created earth. This is the One to be discovered at center, the foundation of all creation and the true basis of all reality. And this One, the God of creation and prophets who is in Jesus Christ reconciling the world to itself, can be our God, if we say *yes*. This One calls you, with the vision it gives you of itself, to hold all others and the whole creation with deep affection, the affection of the mother who loves and defends. This is the call to justice and community found at the center of grace. Although it does not lead to individualism, it is your uniquely individual experience of God when grace claims you as its own, God's child, brother, and sister of all.

In the embrace of Grace we are in moments of mystery and clarity that are of the experience willed by the pure heart. It is a time of being alone and knowing that one is not now or ever will be alone. It is a time of transcending individual experience that reveals the interrelatedness of all persons, creatures, and creation. It is a time of ultimate religious experience that leaves one with no choice but to freely, fully, and forever love God. It is a time that provides at the same time the clearest understanding of the interdependence of all beings from which the commandment to love thy neighbor as self originates.

The mystical experience is neither the end nor purpose of Christian life. It is a gift of grace that comes to those who seek to know and be faithful to God at the center. This guided journey has been written in an effort to expand and add to truths discovered through experience in the realm where the mystery of God's grace informs. It is written with individual seekers in mind but more specifically as a resource for inclusive evangelical churches as they encourage people on their spiritual journeys.

SECTION II

Components of Contemplation: The Spiritual Life of an Inclusive Evangelical

CHAPTER 8

Listening: The Beginning of Spiritual Insight

Let anyone with ears listen!

Jesus, Matthew 11:15

Contemplation is the practice of being open to God. God, the foundation of reality, the dynamic compassion within every heart's beat and longing, is to be found in all times and places; therefore the contemplative practice of an inclusive evangelical will not withdraw from the world but will seek ways to be fully alive and aware within the world. The reality of God is found in waiting more easily than initiating, in listening more frequently than in speaking, in prayer more often than in pronouncement, in reverence rather than control. Once found and responded to faithfully God will encourage our initiating, our speaking, our pronouncements, and help us in those things for which we are accountable as stewards. The skills of contemplation discussed here are designed to meet seekers where they are and aid them in building bridges of contemplative practice that will cross from self-centered lives to God-centered lives, their conversion. We begin with the contemplative practice of listening.

Learning to listen is one way to begin developing spiritual insight. It is opening to hearing and thus connecting with another outside of ourselves. By listening we open to the possibility of meeting persons with respect, even reverence that leads to compassionate and creative possibilities for those meeting and being met. This is the quality of relationship Martin Buber calls "I-Thou." Not to listen is the essence of the second of Buber's two basic word pairs, "I-It." To listen may not always be rewarded with hearing but it is an attitude that maximizes what hearing can be done. An attitude of listening is an attitude of faith. It believes in the "thouness" of the other. It is prerequisite to hearing. To listen also maximizes being heard. Your willingness to be with another so as to allow that person room for expression contributes to an atmosphere that encourages the other's openness to you. Listening is basic to relationship with nature, with other people, with yourself, and with God.

It is fair to ask if this means that a deaf person is thus cut off from all relationship. The answer is obviously no. The question illustrates that there are more ways of hearing than with our ears. I use listening as a symbol for focused attention upon another that includes all the functions of perception we possess. Sight and hearing are the most obvious of these. All forms of perception, even what has been called extrasensory perception, are important and available to each of us to be used for listening. Listening is a prelude to, and is vital to, relationship and involves all attention one can focus upon another.

Beginning to Listen

To listen to another begins with a decision to try. It is clear that when one is talking, he or she is less apt to be listening. Talking is an active mode. Listening is receptive. There are times when we are appropriately active. In our hurried and verbal culture there are far fewer times when we choose to be receptive.

What is said is often screened through our expectations of what is going to be said and our own feelings about the person and circumstances in which the speaking takes place. It will help us to hear if we can learn to identify our expectations and listen for their confirmation or denial from the one to whom we are listening. Direct inquiries regarding our expectations are the clearest way to gain clarification.

In the relationship between Jesus and his disciples it seems that Jesus was the one making direct inquiries. "Who do people say that I am? Who do you say that I am?" The disciples would have done better listening had they been able to ask Jesus directly who he was. Theirs is a classic example of this nonhearing. They expected him to be the Messiah in the mold of common Jewish understandings of the time, the chosen one of God who would overthrow the Romans and establish God's realm in their midst. In other words, they expected him to meet their needs. Jesus was speaking of a realm other than the one they had been taught to expect. He had to be crucified for them to be convinced that their expectations, their understanding of their needs and their satisfaction, had been wrong. His resurrection was, among other things, the dawning awareness within his followers that he was speaking of something other than what they expected. They had to rethink all of what he had taught them and hear the message again. The realm of God was not to be one of worldly might but one of heavenly compassion understood and reflected in men and women disposed to receptive ways.

That the disciples didn't hear Jesus until after his death, and even then without full clarity, is not uncommon. Many significant persons in our lives, often parents, are not clearly heard or recognized until after a distinct separation, even death. Still, it is possible to hear far more of what we are saying to one another while we are alive and with one another than a casual attitude toward listening will allow. Is anyone ever fully heard? Perhaps only by God.

Listening to a Person as a Work of Art

Poetry is a good metaphor for illustrating listening to people. In order to hear a poem we must listen, listen, wait, and listen again. We need to consider each word and each punctuation mark with care to find, as best we can, what the poet is saying. We will never know all of the poet's inferences but we can know far more by taking care to listen than we possibly could know in a quick reading. As we listen we realize that we are hearing familiar ideas and, if we are honest, will recognize that many are our ideas projected upon the word symbols as well as ideas provided by the poet. This intermingling of our thoughts and the poet's is not inappropriate, but it is important to remember that a portion of what we are hearing is ourselves. In the case of a poem we do not have the poet near to verify meaning. Nor, as artwork, would the poet necessarily want to verify meaning. Rather, the artist asks us to engage in the work and be co-creators, adding our meaning after we have given full consideration to his or hers.

Every person is a work of art. We do not err much to look at a poem and see instruction for listening to people. Here are two poems by Rainer Maria Rilke as illustration. Read them quickly and you may find something, but I wager that it will not be nearly as much as is there to be found. Read them again, aloud this time, and more will come to consciousness. Then wait, reflect, and read the poem a final time. A further action on your part will simulate verification with the poet. Discuss the poem with someone who has taken the same care in reading it to see what they hear and feel.

From the "Fifteenth Sonnet" of *The Sonnets to Orpheus,*[1]

Breath, you invisible poem!
Steady sheer exchange between the cosmos
and our being. Counterpoise
in which I rhythmically become.

Single wave whose
gradual sea I am; sparest
of all possible seas—
winning the universe.

How many regions in space have been
inside me already. Many winds
are like my son.

You, air, still full of places once mine,
do you know me? You, once
my words' sphere, leaf, and smooth rind.

From "The Ninth Elegy" in *Duino Elegies,*[2]

Why, when this short span of life could
be spent like the laurel, a little darker than
all the other green,
the edge of each leaf fluted
with small waves (life the wind's smile)
—why, then did we have to be human and,
shunning destiny, long for destiny?
Oh not because happiness,
that quick profit of impending loss,
really exists.
Not out of curiosity, not just to
exercise the heart—

that could be in the laurel too . . .
But because being here means so much,
and because all this here and now,
vanishing so quickly,
seems to need us
and strangely concerns us.
Us, the vanishing ones.
ONCE, each, only ONCE.
ONCE and no more.
And us too, ONCE. Never again.
But to have been ONCE,
even if only ONCE,
to have been on EARTH just ONCE—
that's irrevocable.

My initial response to these poems was frustrated incredulity coupled with the experience of being touched by the beauty of truth. I knew that something important was being said but at a level below full rational perception. I couldn't get my mind around them easily. Reading them a second time and then a third time—aloud—helped. Reading poetry aloud always provides me with greater insight. Talking about a poem, another way to verbalize it, brings more clarity if the conversation is open to the perspectives from both parties. In the process my eyes were opened to something of Rilke's meaning and mine. I want to be careful holding these opinions, however, because if they become too rigid they will violate the creative nature of the poetry. As art, people and poetry are not static. Understanding changes and clarifies, clouds and dissolves, but is never complete. Each time I read these poems, having given them enough time and attention to become acquainted, I find truth—always old truth reaffirmed, sometimes new truth—and suggested variations that challenge previous assumptions. I am richer for having encountered them; upon setting them down, I can judge that the considerable energy involved in engaging them was well rewarded by the reality relinquished.

Again I suggest that such an encounter with a poem is similar in many ways to encountering a person. Each encounter is pregnant with revelation when we assume a receptive mode and listen with focused attention. The truth and beauty that each encounter can reveal are gained only after careful attention is paid to the unique person encountered.

On the matter of uniqueness and variety, inevitably encountered when we consider each person as an individual, we are enlightened by the counsel of C. S. Lewis to his literary correspondent, Malcolm, to whom he addresses his letters in his book, *Letters to Malcolm: Chiefly on Prayer.*[3] Lewis is commenting upon Rose Macaulay, a woman who evidently has a passion for collecting written prayers. He says,

> But though, like you, staggered, I was not, like you, repelled. One reason is that I had—and you hadn't—the luck to meet her. Make no mistake. She was the right sort; one of the most civilized people I ever knew. The other reason, as I have so often told you, is that you are a bigot. Broaden your mind, Malcolm, broaden your mind! It takes all sorts to make a world; or a church. This may be even truer of the church. If grace perfects nature it must expand all our natures into the full richness of the diversity which God intended when He made them, and Heaven will display far more variety than Hell.

If we listen carelessly we can too easily commit the error of categorizing an individual, which robs the person of individuality and seals off the truth offered. If we do not listen fully, we end up projecting our assumptions upon the person based on our own predispositions and initial impressions. This process of shallow listening and categorizing leads to inaccuracy, bigotry, and alienation.

Hearing the Unconscious

Theodore Reik, a psychoanalyst, wrote a book in 1948 called *Listening with the Third Ear.* The third ear to which he referred is in the unconscious. It is the ability to tune into the intuitive responses that present themselves unannounced. Reik traces his respect for this third ear to a conversation he had with Sigmund Freud in Vienna when Reik was one of his students. He writes,

> One evening I ran into the great man on his daily walk along the Ringstrasse in Vienna, and walked home with him. Friendly as always, he asked me about my plans and I told him of my problems. . . . Of course, I hoped Freud would give me advice or resolve my doubts. "I can only tell you of my personal experience," he said. "When making a decision of minor importance, I have always found

it advantageous to consider all the pros and cons. In vital matters, however, such as the choice of a mate or a profession, the decision should come from the unconscious, from somewhere within ourselves. In the important decisions of our personal life, we should be governed, I think, by the deep needs of our nature."[4]

In Reik's reporting of his counseling techniques he makes a great deal of the insights that come to him tangentially from his unconscious. There could well be a case made for calling that source of information a second voice. Reik calls for a third ear to hear it. The speaking of the unconscious is of such a nature that it seems to come from beyond or through us. Listening for and trusting the speaking is the important point Reik makes; I call attention to it for our consideration of listening. There will be much more for us to consider about the voice that speaks from within as we continue with the other ways of exercising spiritual perception, particularly through our dreams. The point made here is that in listening closely to what another has to tell us in the many ways an individual has of speaking, i.e., verbal, nonverbal, psychically, it is good to listen as well to the seemingly unrelated responses that are triggered within us.

Reik illustrates this phenomenon by telling of a line from *Hamlet* that came into his mind as he listened to a patient. He was able to equate the circumstance of the character speaking the line in the play with the situation of his patient, even though the patient had not given evidence that such a connection could logically be made. Upon pursuing the possibility, Reik reports that indeed there emerged clear evidence that his unconscious was perceiving a genuine but until then undisclosed dynamic.

Admittedly this is tricky business and can get into what Carl Jung and others have called *projection*. Projection is our unconscious or repressed self, containing vulnerabilities, fears, and fantasies, projected as if from a slide or movie projector upon the individual we see. Our projections are thought to be an accurate picture of the one projected upon. Our unacknowledged aspect is recognized in the acts or words of another—not recognized as our projection, but identified as an attribute of the other. This is very easy to do and, in fact, is done regularly by most of us. It can block hearing. To listen well we must confirm our perceptions with the one perceived. If they deny ownership of our observations we will do well to consider that what is being discussed is at least as likely to be our projection as their unfaced attribute.

I encourage you to check out your hunches, your perceptions with the person with whom you are engaged in conversation or with another with whom you are sharing an experience. We all have intuitive perceptive abilities, but it takes training to develop them. These intuitive skills are gifts of perception that can aid you in hearing and understanding another person to a far greater degree than would be the case if you were without them. Be careful to confirm their accuracy with the other person. Intuitive skills are similarly effective in helping us to hear ourselves and God.

Listening Training

Listening is so important for quality relationships with God, neighbor, and self that intentional development of listening skills deserves time and effort. It is such a central aspect of religious attitude and experience that churches would do well to offer repeated opportunities for listening training groups to form and help one another. The following categories of listening were developed for use in such groups.

1. Nonverbal Listening

We have learned that the hardest obstacle to remove from the listening process is ourselves. In a class to improve listening various skills are practiced that move us aside to facilitate listening to the other. The skills are exaggerated because they are in a laboratory setting, but they work. The first and most other-focused skill is silent response. Eye contact is established, body attention is given as well as mind attention. Without speaking response is given to what the speaker is saying. In this exercise we encourage noises such as "oh!" "umm," "humm?" and various grunts and groans. Nonverbal responses such as smiles, tears, and gestures are encouraged. The fewer words spoken by the listener the better. It sounds hard to do. The class members wonder how they can do it. They see themselves being the fool, waiting mutely for something to begin, enduring awkward pauses, squirming in their seats. Sometimes a question is needed to prime the verbal pump of the speaker. But it is surprising how little a speaker needs from a listener in the way of words when full attention is being paid. It is not uncommon to have someone comment after they have been listened to by someone who intentionally used nonverbal responses and very few words that it was a wonderful conversation. And in fact it was.

2. Echoing

The second skill we work on is the echo response. It is still very much focused upon the speaker but involves the listener in more verbal interaction. The response of the listener to the statements of the speaker is for confirmation that he is being heard or, if the echo is formed as a question, clarification. It is phrased in a restatement, or echo, of what the listener thinks he or she heard being said. For instance, if the speaker is talking about a hard time she was having with her child and says, "I can't do anything with that child," the listener responds with full attention accorded the person listened to by saying, "You can't do anything with your child." Again, it can be said as a statement or a question but the effect is similar. The person listened to is pleased to be heard and encouraged to continue with the story.

3. Clarification: Details

This response is most often in the form of a question. It is important that the listener not get lost in the story being heard, even though it is not unusual that for one reason or another he or she misses an important point. Since this can block listening, a question of clarification is needed. Time taken by the listener to clarify the details of the story confirms the listener's interest and keeps the listening focused.

4. Clarification: Feelings

All stories contain many levels of feelings. Being able to talk about them with someone can be a gift of self-understanding and mutual acceptance. A convenient summary of possible feelings are the four words *mad*, *glad*, *sad*, and *scared*. Sensing feelings from the speaker can bring the conversation to deeper levels of insight and caring if the listener can clarify the tone. Questions from the listener that leave the description of the speaker's feelings to the speaker are best. Comments such as "You have a lot of feeling about this" enable the speaker to pursue examining his or her emotions. A clarifying question addressed to a specific emotional tone can be used but needs to be spoken so as to keep the definition with the speaker. Asking if the speaker was mad, sad, glad, or scared is a possible way to clarify feelings. With this response listening moves into more intimate levels of relationship, which may or may not be appropriate. It is necessary to point out both here and in a listening class that these responses are not typical cocktail party or coffee break responses. They lead quickly to a level of intimacy, particularly when feelings become part of the conversation, that most people do not bargain for in casual contact. Part of responsible listening is to recognize the assumptions of the circumstances of a conversation and honor them. It could be, however, that someone wants to talk at a deeper level than party conversation. A question clarifying that possibility is appropriate and acts as an agreement to move to a deeper level of relationship. For example, one might ask, "Are you hurting?" If that perception is confirmed, the next question is, "Do you want to talk to me about it?" Of course if *you* don't want to talk about it you would not respond with your perception. Some situations are not right, for reasons of time or circumstance, to pursue a conversation into I-Thou dimensions. It is such times when you might opt for what Harvey Cox in *Secular City* calls "I-You" relations—where you recognize that if time and situation allowed, you would pursue a more intimate level of conversation. Behind the I-You relation is the acknowledgment that the thou of the individual is honored but not engaged at that time.

Listening skills are valuable for aiding others in their need to be heard. It is astounding how much healing can be accomplished if someone in pain can find another who is sensitive enough to hear the story through and let the speaker come to his/her own solutions. There are occasions when advice is in order but not nearly as often as we advice-givers would like to think. Most of the answers needed and appropriate to the problems encountered are already present in the troubled persons. They need empathy to release the solutions they possess. Upon discovery of these solutions released in the listening process, great joy and deepened friendship are shared by both members of the conversation.

5. Identifying With

There are two more responses we discuss in our listening class. They involve increasingly more participation by the listener and thus are both more similar to "normal" conversation, making it difficult to keep focused upon the one being listened to. The fifth response is to identify with the remarks of the person speaking and cite similar incidents in your experience. A common direction for a conversation to go when one tries this response is for the listener to becoming the one being listened to. This is to be expected in day-to-day conversations. It is understood that both parties to a conversation have the right to contribute their own experiences and conclusions. The point made here, however, is that it is not the best way for you to hear other people. The most common method used in conversations to take the focus from another and put it on yourself is to identify. Often-heard transitional statements in the shift of attention include "I know just what you mean," "Just the other day . . . ," and "That reminds me of the time. . . . " You, of course, have a right to be heard, but we are talking about the development of listening skills. If, by more sensitive listening, you become more aware of the state of being of another person, you will also be more able to know when it is appropriate for you to introduce your concern and ask to be heard. This will result in clearer communication all around.

6. Advice

The sixth response is common sense and necessary if one is listening in an I-thou relationship. If a person is telling you about a problem and you care about the person to whom you are listening, it is appropriate for you to consider giving advice at some point in the conversation. Before advice is given, however, be sure that it is wanted, which can be done by simply asking. Even if advice is wanted it should not be given too quickly. One difficulty with given advice is that a listener can be tempted to minimize a problem by offering a solution too quickly, before the one being listened to has had a good opportunity to consider his or her own solution, opportunity gained more in giving full expression to the need than in planning a solution. An answer or advice too quickly offered by the listener could be because of anxiety generated in him or her by the problem. It is just as often the case that advice is given too quickly because of the listener's need to be an answer-giver. For whatever reason, advice given too quickly is not good listening.

What you will discover as you develop listening skills is what Martin Buber calls reciprocity. His words are translated from the original German by Walter Kaufmann as follows:

> Relation is reciprocity. My [Thou] acts on me as I act on it. Our students teach us, our works form us. The "wicked" become a revelation when they are touched by the sacred basic word [I-Thou]. How we are educated by children, by animals! Inscrutably involved, we live in the currents of universal reciprocity.[5]

In a listening course we consider the above responses and work on developing them one at a time. This is done frequently in groups of three. One member of the group agrees to be an observer and the other two act as speaker and listener. Generally we will not suggest a topic for conversation; rather, we ask people to begin talking about their day and its events. One of the early discoveries in listening training is that any event in a person's life is an opening to much more of that person's life. A session can last for any period of time, but five minutes of conversation between the listener and speaker is adequate. Then they turn to the observer for her or his observations. After each triad member has had a chance to function in each role (generally about thirty minutes is enough time), the triads return to the larger group. Reports from the triads provide additional learning. Both our listening skills and lives are enriched—the former through the listening training and the latter by the relationships deepened through the class process.

It has been found that working with the first three responses one at a time is the best way to understand and learn them. We encourage each response to be worked on in relationships inside and outside of the class. The class members are asked to try their listening skills at home, on their jobs, with their friends. The discussion of these efforts begins each session.

People need not be professional counselors to help one another learn to listen. What they do need is to be willing to speak frankly to one another from the observer role. Without that objective perspective and the frank critique of skills, the learning process is considerably slowed.

Meditation as Listening

A helpful step in developing listening skills is learning how to make room. What this amounts to is turning down the voices of the activities of life so that the more subtle and softer voices of intuitive nature can be heard. We need to set aside time for "quieting" to make room for imaginative and intuitive expression. As we learn to listen to these expressions, they will find their way with greater frequency into our conscious awareness. The spiritual guides of the East have given us their meditative disciplines, and those interested in developing these skills more thoroughly would do well to look to the literature in these areas. For our purposes I turn our attention to the writings of physician and researcher Herbert Benson. Here is an example of the scientific mind giving serious consideration to an intuitive skill. The result is clear, precise, unbiased, albeit one dimensional, but it gives us helpful facts and directions for our own meditative practices. So, with a word of thanks to Dr. Benson for the facts and a word of encouragement to you to experience meditation first hand, let's consider what he has to teach us.

In *The Relaxation Response*[6] Benson reports the effects of meditation, position, and method. His method is similar to that of transcendental meditation with a variation regarding a mantra. His conclusions are that the object of preoccupation during meditation is not as important as the result of preoccupation, i.e., focused attention to reduce "mind wandering." His recommendation is that the word *one* is just as good as any sound used as a mantra or repeated word to focus attention during mediational centering down. His recommendations for developing what he calls the relaxation response are as follows:

1. A Quiet Environment
2. A Mental Device
    To shift the mind from logical, externally oriented thought, there should be a constant stimulus: a sound, word, or phrase repeated silently or aloud; or fixed gazing at an object. Your eyes are usually closed if you are using a repeated sound or word. Attention to the normal rhythm of breathing is also useful and enhances the repetition of the sound or the word.
3. A Passive Attitude
    When distracting thoughts occur, they are to be disregarded

and attention redirected to the repetition or gazing; *you should not worry about how well you are performing the technique.* Adopt a "let it happen" attitude.
4. A Comfortable Position

Benson's study, conducted under the auspices of the Harvard Medical School at the Beth Israel Hospital in Boston, showed that the daily practice of this technique for a period of ten to twenty minutes reduced hypertension and anxiety levels.

It may be that Benson arrived at the use of the word *one* for attention focusing by random selection. And it may be that the meaning of the word has little to do with the degree of relaxation attained. It is interesting for us to recognize that "one" is the primary symbol of the unity that is the full realization of the mystical insight. Be that as it may, Benson has aided us by presenting a simple process for making room, quieting the active mode within ourselves.

Another practice of receptive waiting is to breathe in through your nose and exhale through your mouth, attempting to count each breath until quieted. This can be six counts one day, twelve the next, or four the next. I count until quieted. Following the count, I frequently move into concentration upon the breath with an image of God's peace coming in to me when inhaling and extending from me when exhaling. I use the word *shalom* as a mantra, chanting it in two syllables on the exhale. Following the chanting, a period determined by how long it takes me to move into a quieted place of unity, I wait there and consider whomever I remember, imagining the light of God's peace enveloping them. This is a form of prayer. Thanks and praise of God whose light shines in the face of Jesus Christ concludes the time of prayer and meditation. In telling of my own practice I have gone beyond discussing "making room" and moved into some aspects of prayer that will be discussed later. What I hope to communicate by these examples of meditation is that there is no set way to meditate, but there are similarities in the ways discussed. It seems that the discipline of emptying one's mind does facilitate openness to the quieting and centering energies that come from the intuitive aspects of the mind. I would encourage you to experiment with your own style and mantra to the end of making room.

Once you have found your way to a quiet place within, it should be easier to travel that way more often. When it becomes a familiar path you can travel it easily and quickly so that just a few deep breaths may lead you there. In this quietness there is room for intuitive expression, for the imagination to unlimber itself.

There are many analogies for this process of finding room, what I like to call receptive waiting. One I have referred to already is called "centering" and it comes from the vocabulary of the potter. M. C. Richards calls her book *Centering*, which begins with these words relevant to our thoughts:

> Centering: that act which precedes all others on the potter's wheel. The bringing of the clay into a spinning, unwobbling pivot, which will then be free to take innumerable shapes as potter and clay press against each other. The firm, tender, sensitive pressure which yields as much as it asserts.
>
> It is like a handclasp between two living hands, receiving the greeting at the very moment that they give it. It is this speech between the hand and the clay that makes me think of dialogue. And it is a language far more interesting than the spoken vocabulary which tries to describe it, for it is spoken not by the tongue and lips but by the whole body, by the whole person, speaking and listening. And with listening too, it seems to me, it is not the ear that hears, it is not the physical organ that performs that act of inner receptivity. It is the total person who hears. Sometimes the skin seems to be the best listener, as it prickles and thrills, say to a sound or a silence or the fantasy, the imagination: how it bursts into inner pictures as it listens and then responds by pressing its language, its forms, into the listening clay. To be open to what we hear, to be open in what we say.[7]

Listening Is Spiritual Practice

One concluding word about listening: A receptive attitude toward others, self, and God, which is the essence of listening, is a central aspect of spiritual practice. Much can and will be said about prayer, dreams, mystical experience, servant living, and other aspects of the spiritual experience and life. But simple listening with its openness to and valuing of others, with its patience and faith that there is something of worth to be heard in the other/Other is prelude to humility, wisdom, and wonder. It is an indispensable aspect of meeting God, neighbor, and self.

CHAPTER 9

Imagination: The Bridge from Fact to Truth

You hear a Beethoven symphony in the concert hall. If you come home to discuss the conductor or the details of the performance, it may be interesting. But if you come home vaguely discontented with yourself, aware deep down of the contrast between the commonness or even banality of your life and the world into which Beethoven has given you a glimpse, then your imagination, the creative part of you, has been touched. A chain reaction may be beginning that may end in turning your life upside down. *Imagination:* here is the word which to me comes nearest to being adequate for this mysterious creative force. For imagination is the faculty by virtue of which man is created in the *image* of God.

—Harold Clarke Goddard
Alphabet of the Imagination[1]

Imagination is the capacity with which one responds to the "Deep" of creation that calls to the "deep" within each of us (Ps. 42:7). When the Truth of existence beckons, exciting the deep need within us to find harmony with it in our understanding and behavior, our imagination is our means of conceptualization and response. Truth is understood in this sense as essence, essence which exists in all things in dimensions that exceed our logical capacities to define, yet within our intuitive capacities to understand. Truth is diminished by certainty, enlivened by imagination.

The ascendancy of regard for the rational in our Western thought processes has been for good reasons. Logic, order, objective analysis, the demand for the proof of the scientific process all are necessary correctives to the chaos of the powerlessness individuals feel in wilderness settings, be they the wilds of superstition, oppressive authoritarianism, or frontier exploration. Yet imagination has saved me from chaos as often as has rationality.

I recall a desperate night when I was agonizing over the suicide of a young friend, a freshman at Harvard University, with all the promise for human realization of any young man I have known. I called to my God complaining that I could not hold the world on my shoulders any longer, the weight was more than I could stand. I stood alone in my study, bent over as Atlas, my palms open upward behind my neck bearing an imaginary globe, a world of responsibility and grief. The world and its weight pressed me to my knees and threatened to crush me. God answered and said, "Let go." "If I let go it will fall," I protested. God, in a silent voice, assured me. "You are not holding up the world. I am." It was then that I realized that my fear was deeper. "God, if I let go I will fall." "Let go," God replied. "I am holding you too."

Prayer. It was prayer that I expressed and an answer to prayer that I experienced. And it was through imagination that the truth of both my condition and our God were expressed and clarified. Imagination is essential to religious experience and understanding.

The Bible as Imaginative Literature

Imagination is essential to explore the experience of others found in religious literature. With all of the benefit to be derived from modern rational scholarship of the Bible, the Truth to be found in it is hidden from those who rely entirely upon objective interpretation of the scriptures. This is just as true for the scholars of modern biblical criticism as it is for those who insist upon reading scriptures literally. To understand that religious literature is more like poetry than arithmetic allows the reader to explore Truth rather than fact. Despite efforts within biblical scholarship to "demythologize" the Bible, it is understanding the Bible as myth that leads us to its Truth. Myth is not the opposite of truth even though it is not factual. That is, it is not necessarily an accurate account of a previous happening as told by an unbiased observer. Myth is a story set in time that contains the reality it would have us know, which is for all time. The details of the story are symbol and fact. They are the facts of the story but symbols of the timeless Truth they tell, Truth that is beyond full definition, never fully told in a thousand stories. The myth, for example, of the nativity of Jesus found primarily in the gospel of Luke and completed in Matthew, need not be defended as literally true to be Truth. To discard the Virgin Birth because it is not considered to be literally true or, on the other hand, insist that it must be literally true or it has no Truth, insulates the seeker from the Truth the myth contains. It is a multidimensional Truth that speaks of Jesus and Mary. It can speak of human existence and divinity, of aspects of maleness and/or femaleness, and can address questions and needs of the human spirit that we have not yet recognized. To limit the Truth of the myth to the objective detail of the story, Mary, a virgin, was impregnated by the Holy One and not by Joseph or any other mortal, denies the multidimensional possibilities of understanding the Truth of Jesus and Mary imagination has and has yet to reveal. Imagination allows us the latitude to explore the mystery of the myth and find meaning outside of the rigid limitations imposed by belief in truth as fact alone. Imagination does not limit perspectives but increases them much as facets on a diamond are cut to maximize the light the gem is able to reflect.

There is a place for facts in religious thought. Logic and rational reasoning provide a perspective upon reality that cannot be ignored or abandoned. But there is more Truth to be found in symbol and myth than literal interpretation alone and more Truth to be found in the inquiry that values both than one that chooses either one or the other.

Imagination Binds Together With Light

Imagination has been a dominant preoccupation of Harold Clarke Goddard and is affirmed in a collection of his literary essays entitled *Alphabet of the Imagination*. Goddard has a high regard for the romantics of English literature who challenged what they saw as sterility in the dominant rationality of the Enlightenment. Chief among these was William Blake who wrote:

God appears and God is Light
To those poor Souls who dwell in Night,
But does a Human Form Display
To those who Dwell in Realms of day.[2]

Is Blake saying that for those in the darkness that the Light itself is God, but for those who are familiar with Light, who dwell in day, that those things illuminated by the Light reveal God as well? Perhaps. One of the gifts and challenges of Blake's writing is that the reader's imagination is engaged. Is God in all human forms for Blake? Knowing his art, one would suspect so, but his imagination leads us to consider the incarnation as well. Exploring Blake's inspiration and expression affirms the reader that he would agree with Goddard who said, "As the intellect cuts apart, so the imagination binds together"[3]

In the book of Revelation John of Patmos has a vision of great imagination in which he sees a figure of

> one like a son of man clothed with a long robe and with a golden girdle round his breast; his head and his hair were white as white wool, white as snow; his eyes were like a flame of fire, his feet were like burnished bronze refined as in a furnace, and his voice was like the sound of many waters; in his right hand he held seven stars, from his mouth issued a sharp two-edged sword, and his face was like the sun shining in full strength. (Rev. 1:13b–16)

What would one do in the face of such power, in the presence of an image with radiance from its face as the sun into which we cannot look without losing our sight? We would probably do what John did—fall down before it and wait for whatever it chose to do. He played dead. In this position of powerlessness, with dread and awe in equal portions flowing through him, he felt the touch of a hand and heard these words:

> Do not be afraid; I am the first and the last, and the living one. I was dead, and see, I am alive forever and ever; and I have the keys of Death and Hades. Now write what you have seen, what is, and what is to take place after this. (Rev. 1:17b–19)

It is this vision from which come the words of Revelation 3:20: "Listen! I am standing at the door knocking; if you hear my voice and open the door, I will come in to you and eat with you, and you with me." If we open the door the breath of God, the wind of Spirit will blow upon our smoldering soul, bringing it first to glowing brilliance and then to leaping flame, the flame of life that burns in all and in which all are one. Can you hear, see, feel similarity in this essential Blake?

> Tiger! Tiger! burning bright
> In the forests of the night.[4]

Imagination is the product of our mental abilities blown upon by Spirit wind that comes through us rather than from us. There is some discussion regarding the residence and identity of this wind. There was no question in the mind of Wordsworth or Blake, however, that the creative capacity is within but dependent upon inspiration from beyond for its manifest expression as imagination. In my own efforts at poetry and any creative expressions that look to imagination for shaping, there has been a clear sense that I function as channel of expression that is fully me yet from beyond myself.

So imagination is important to me and to many others as well. It is a process all of us experience but which most of us have relegated to artistic types or children. Yet, I contend that it is a gift to us from the beginning, the exercise of which adds to our vision, expands our experience, relates us to each one and all things most essentially and shows us the way to see God. It is not an end in itself. It is a way of being that can unite us with all and will not leave us content to live in isolation. We can use imagination for less than altruistic purposes but we cannot move with clarity and effective deeds into relationship with others and all of life without exercising the imagination given us. Inviting you, then, to continue in the exploration and development of your spiritual capacities, we will consider how imagination is encouraged and implemented in various exercises and disciplines.

Each of us uses imagination in most areas of our lives. It may be creative thought regarding the solution to some mechanical problem or insight concerning the personality of a friend. It may be in an artistic effort, such as painting, writing, sculpting. A parent, a student, a professional person, a craftsman, a street person dedicated to personal survival—all of these call for some degree of imaginative thought. Most of us know the satisfying experience of having tried a new thought or solution and seen its unique contribution. In areas of our lives where we feel some confidence we can risk letting go more easily and allow imagination to introduce new possibilities. In areas where we are less confident we prefer control over our behavior and attempt to minimize the risks of ridicule or embarrassment. This control can hold back new possibilities that imagination could introduce. The issue is not best thought of as either/or. One need not give up all control (some would prefer to call it restraint) in order to give freer expression to imagination. We each need to make our own decisions about when and how we experiment with freer imaginative expression. In our secular culture, where high value is placed upon control, most err on the side of not giving one's imagination a more free reign to the detriment of our fuller spiritual realization and God's greater purposes for our lives.

Exercises Encouraging Imagination In Spiritual Understanding

Learning to trust your imagination is an important step in developing skills in spiritual insight. To explore the symbols of faith requires listening, open consideration, imaginative exploration, respect for the hunches and ideas that seem to come out of the air. To pray you need to let your thoughts and words explore your feelings as well as your ideas and listen creatively for answers that come in unexpected forms and signs. Bible study is wonderfully rich when free association and role playing accompany solid scholarship. Finally, to have faith in something is to allow one's imagination to engage and open faith's object to dimensions that exceed our knowing yet are allowed in our believing.

1. Putting Yourself There: Imaginative Bible Study

Choose a section of the Bible that you want to involve yourself with and read it through. As you read, let your imagination roam freely over the actors and setting of the scene you encounter. Having completed the passage, go back and construct the scene, set the stage. Describe the room in which the action takes place or the look of the countryside. Think about temperature, humidity, weather. Put yourself in the setting and feel it.

Now select the principal characters and describe them one by one. Where have they been before arriving on this scene? What are they wearing? What is at issue for them in this particular moment? Close your eyes and give them faces, complexions, stature. Add whatever other props and detail are necessary and then play out the scene. Use the words of the narrative but add others that may be necessary in your imagined circumstances, and in the process experience the action and reaction of the individuals involved. You can do this alone, or, better, with others.

After having played through the scene, refer to a good Bible commentary and read what the persons who wrote there have to say about the same scene. They will have some important data to contribute, but they are no more an authority on the human dimension than you. Having added to your script with the input of commentaries you may want to play through the scene again. A final exercise is to note in conversation or in your journal any central impressions, message, or insight that came to you in the process. Often an item of concern that has been on the back burner of your mind will find some perspective through this exercise by virtue of the fact that you have allowed your intuitive skills to move more freely, stimulated by the richness of our biblical resources.

2. Guided Imagery

Two ways of using guided imagery to explore imaginative insight are to be guided by verbal suggestion and by selected music. Both require trust on the part of the travelers, trust of their guide, and trust in their imagination.

Let me illustrate imagery guided by verbal suggestion by setting a scene and providing a script for the guide. The travelers are asked to find a comfortable position, on the floor, in a chair, wherever they feel most secure and free of pressure. Often this means a position facing away from others, far enough removed so that there is no accidental touching that will interrupt the fantasy or begin another. We then breathe deeply and exhale slowly, centering ourselves in the place where we are. The first part of the trip is in the body; the second outside. The travelers are asked to imagine themselves breathing their consciousness out with one easy and prolonged breath and then, hovering above, to look down to view their bodies. After a pause for their own observation, they are asked to let their consciousness move into their body with prolonged inhaling of air into the lungs. I invite them then to pass through the lungs with fresh oxygen and into their bloodstream and move where they wish, listening to the beat of the heart get louder or softer as they move nearer to or farther from it. It is suggested that they explore from top to bottom. After a few minutes of silence to allow whatever movement in themselves they want, they are asked to move back into their lungs and out with the next exhalation. Above themselves they are then introduced to the possibility of moving around the world at any speed they wish observing all that is happening below. They are invited to move until they find a place where they would like to stop and spend some time. Time is allowed for that journey. I then ask who they find at the location of their visit. More directed suggestions can be given by the guide. The travelers can be asked to move across the face of the earth and consider the millions of people on it and the various conditions in which they find them. They can be asked to look for Jesus with or in the people and places to which they travel. After a period of time they are encouraged to move back to the space above the room in which we are located, then into the room, and finally, with a long inhale, back into their own body, returning consciousness to its home. It often takes many minutes after returning into ourselves to move again and re-enter relationship with others in the room. Following these trips, we talk them over and discuss various experiences of the body and the far-ranging journey. Journeys such as this can lead to important self and group insights as well as shared experience.

My first experience of guided imagery to music was with a group of eight in one room made comfortable with rugs, pillows, sofas, and trusting people. Music taped for the purpose was used, but first we were assigned a partner for the trip. We then took turns acting as recorder of verbal responses for the other person's trip. The music played for approximately twenty minute intervals. We began with deep breaths and quieting moments. The music was then started and the traveler told the recorder what the music brought to mind. The recorder listened carefully and asked an occasional clarifying question if she or he did not understand what the traveler was saying. Essentially the traveler described the settings that the music suggested and followed, as in a dream, a sequence of experiences or observations that imagination suggested. Following a brief interval for refreshment the partners exchanged positions and the traveler was now the recorder and vice versa. In both cases the traveler assumed whatever physical position seemed most comfortable to him or her.

After the second trip the partners talked with one another about their experience, using the recorder's notes as a reminder. This experience of imagination was valuable in and of itself, as are all experiences of imagination. It had additional value in that it allowed the participants to find feelings, opinions, suggestions from the imagination that spoke to them about interests, inclinations, and, sometimes, major concerns. The final gift of experience is the value of verbalizing our imagining with another person, who in turn trusts us with his or hers.

For those not used to moving self-consciously into the realm of imagination it is helpful to try to keep your expectations, both negative and positive, minimal. A common error is to expect great insight or great embarrassment resulting from the risking of vulnerability when loosening your grip on self-control. Sometimes the insights of imaginative experience are subtle, on occasion powerful. One thing is constant, however: the less demanding you are of the experience, the freer you will be to perceive and receive the gift it has to offer. One group of which I was a part used imagery as a method of guided meditation. Our leader suggested that we imagine a mountain that we had to climb; upon reaching the summit we would find Jesus. We were then left to pursue the journey as our imagination and inclination allowed. Some did not feel comfortable with the suggestions and used the time for their own purposes. Others tried to make the journey but found themselves resisting the suggestion that it had to be Jesus on top and so refused to climb all the way. Others climbed but knew that it wouldn't be Jesus and found another heroic figure; some found a wise old man, others a woman. Some could accept the suggestion and looked forward to meeting Jesus but found that they couldn't bring themselves to go the whole way, finding some resistance within themselves of which they had not been previously aware. Others climbed and engaged with Jesus and asked a question that was a revelation in itself as they heard themselves asking it. Others found significance in the words they heard Jesus speak.

When the meditation was finished there was prolonged conversation dominated in feeling by those who resisted the idea of setting foot on the mountain at all. What was being learned by the group in this process was not only individual insights but freedom in group relations. Each had the freedom to enter the fantasy or not, to the degree he or she wished or was able. It was hardest for those who felt manipulated by the technique. If they did feel manipulated, however, they did the right thing by not participating. The only obligation they have in that situation is to take responsibility for their feelings and learn from their own actions and reactions.

The uses of guided imagery and other techniques of imagination and spiritual development are not to manipulate or usurp responsibility from persons. They are available for those who find the desire in themselves to try them. Developing your intuitive skills is suggested as a way to aid you in learning the language of spirit. There is no guarantee of delivery or clear destination implied in suggesting these exercises. That is between you and the voice within that calls you to new places. What is asked is that you take responsibility for your spiritual journey and work to minimize your preoccupations about where it will take you. After all, God is ultimately the guide who leads you home.

3. Imaginative Movement

There is a special release of energy that comes when connection between imagination and expression is made. This is clearly the case when bodily movements give expression to feelings and ideas that well up from our imagination. Dancing is the easiest example of this.

I am one who is freer to let my body move in response to my feelings when no one else is looking or else in the company of trusted friends. On occasion I venture onto a dance floor and reveal my attempts at the movements that pass as contemporary dance. My own self-consciousness often hinders the free spirit within me from full expression. But, give me the right day, the right music, and a trusting space and I can dance. The gift of the dance is a glorious connection with myself, others, and life.

This sort of exercise, moving to the mood of the music, is similar to the guided imagery to music just spoken of, except that body language is used rather than verbalization. In some ways physical expression is cleaner, i.e., a freer, more direct expression of imagination than words. Words, after all, are symbols while body movement is expression in a primary mode.

Body movement and prayer can be integrated in a liberating way. The problem of self-consciousness is still real, but a retreat setting can minimize this inhibition by virtue of common commitment and circumstance. The Lord's Prayer is a prayer that lends itself to physical expression. One adaptation of the prayer to movement involves three basic body positions and one basic movement of the hands and arms. The prayer is begun with people kneeling, sitting back on their feet with their hands held palms together as in "Praying Hands." As the prayer begins, praying hands are extended upward to the full length of the arms and then parted. The arms are extended and slowly dropped to the sides. On "give us this day . . . " the people move to kneeling with their backs straight. The hands, again in a prayerful position in front of their bodies, are extended up, then out and down again to their sides, arriving there while saying, "deliver us from evil . . . . " Then, as they bring their hands together once more to pray during "for thine is the kingdom . . . ," they stand and extend their hands in the same motion done twice before, dropping them to their sides easily on "Amen."

4. Journals

There are many precedents for spiritual journals. Henry David Thoreau's journal is well known. Quakers have kept journals that have become a resource for many who follow in their way, particularly the journals of George Fox and John Woolman. Keeping a journal requires a regular maintenance and provides information for reflection and perspective. A journal can be a record of dreams or of daily activities, a diary. It can include strictly verbal accounts of actions and reactions or be a collection of images, pictures, symbols drawn by the journalist for his or her purposes, or a scrapbook of bits and pieces, articles and comments clipped for keeping. Essentially a journal is a self-reflective technique.

One problem with intuitive experience is that it fades from memory easily. It wells forth from the unconscious but seems all too ready to sift back down, as water in sand, to its subterranean source. Gifts of imagination such as dreams, insights, inspiration, correlations of meaning, and understandings of relationships seem unusually able to flee memory unless we develop an intentional system for collecting them. A journal is such a system.

The Ira Progoff Intensive Journal method suggested in his book, *At An Intensive Journal Workshop*,[5] has been helpful to individuals in groups I have led. Progoff introduces a technique called "dialogue." This is a method that is simple in form and often helpful, even profound, in use. All journal work begins with a period of quieting, an individually chosen method of centering. The dialogue is between whomever you choose. It is your journal, for your private and personal use, not to be seen by any other than those to whom you choose to read or show. I frequently find myself dialoguing with God, yet I often use the technique to work on difficult interpersonal matters. Dialoguing with God is another way of praying. When working on some other relationship it is prayerful conversation. "Prayerful" does not mean without feelings of anger, frustration, fear, joy, or sorrow. The keeper of the journal writes his or her initials and asks a question or makes a statement. Then the initials of the one with whom you are in dialogue are written and you give your hand over to that one's mind and heart to respond. The give-and-take continues until the journal keeper decides that it is time to conclude. It often seems that a natural conclusion to the conversation is found in the process. Invariably I find that dialoguing in my journal gives me a new perspective upon the relationship or issue I am working on.

Another journal exercise that has been helpful in my experience is what Progoff calls "Stepping Stones." Variations on the exercise have been used, but essentially it amounts to a process of six steps beginning with centering. The second step is to make a list of significant moments in one's life, which Progoff calls stepping stones. These are events that made a difference in the direction your life took. Third, the list of stepping stones (often a number of eight to twelve is encouraged) is reviewed. As the journaler reviews the list, she/he is asked to be attentive to which particular stepping stone holds the most interest at the moment. Which stepping stone, for whatever reason, stimulates a more energized response within you than the others? The fourth phase of the exercise is to expand the most energized stepping stone by writing in detail the story around that event in your life, complete with time, place, people, feelings, and so on. The fifth phase of the exercise is to read over your expanded event and note in the margins your feelings and comments about various aspects of the story. The final step is to reflect as to why this stepping stone has energy for your life at this time.

If journaling is done as a group exercise an opportunity is given for the members to tell the group what they have discovered or are dealing with in their journal work. But the journals are closely guarded for privacy and no one is expected to tell what he or she wrote. Those who choose to tell have often found that the verbalization of their work adds another dimension to their understanding, but it is strictly a volunteer activity.

Believing that God works in and through our imaginations, it is clear to see how journaling is a valuable method of listening and conversation with God, neighbor, and self, a helpful skill in one's spiritual practice.

Imagination Lighting the Way

M. C. Richards understands the way of imagination, what she calls the creative spirit. She writes,

> The creative spirit creates with whatever materials are present. With food, with children, with building blocks, with speech, with thoughts, with pigment, with an umbrella, or a wine glass, or a torch. We are not craftsmen only during studio hours. Any more than [one] is wise only in [one's] library. Or devout only in church. The material is not the sign of the creative feeling for life; of the warmth and sympathy and reference which foster being; techniques are not the sign; "art" is not the sign. The sign is the light that dwells within the act, whatever its nature or its medium.[6]

Light. Let your imagination dwell with this symbol for a moment. "In the beginning God created. . . . The earth was without form and void, and darkness was upon the face of the deep; and the Spirit of God was moving over the face of the waters. And God said, 'Let there be light,' and there was light" (Gen. 1:1–3). Jesus, teaching his followers around the Sea of Galilee, told them, "You are the light of the world" (Matt. 5:14). And in John, Jesus is given to say, "I am the light of the world" (John 8:12). John sings faith in the prologue to the fourth gospel as he tells us, "The light shines in the darkness, and the darkness has not overcome it" (John 1:5).

An idea struck me in a dream. It was a message that we are musical instruments upon which God can play; the music that comes forth is of God and us. Our task is to keep the instrument in tune, ready. All of our senses are a part of the instrument: touch, sight, smell, hearing. They all need to be alert, sensitive, ready to vibrate with the inspiration. Our imaginations, also part of our capacity to make music, need to be flexible, exercised, responsive so that when the Light Maker plays upon us we will respond with all that we have to offer. Our minds are part of our instrument and need to be open to what new things are to be revealed as well as true to what has been learned thus far. Our bodies are part of the instrument and their health is kept for God's purposes, their dance and play part of our light-perpetuating stewardship. In all of this there is delight—for God who makes music upon us, and for us who are created for this purpose: to be part of the music- and light-show God makes in the universe.

Let every sunrise and growing tree be a guide to our spiritual journey. Let every light that shines in scripture and the multiple facets of every person illuminate your understanding of the sacredness of the Creation. Let every darkness be contrast, that light may be more glorious. Allow the birds and animals, the fish and the waters, the mountains and deserts, heavens and earth to be the chorus singing God's praises. With the psalmist, watch the floods clap their hands and hear the hills sing for joy together. Can you imagine the glory of God? Can you speak it, sing it, dance it? It shines as light all about and through us for those who are ready to see.

The fire of William Blake's Tiger, the inner light of the Quakers, the inspiration of John's prologue that was the Word, the Christ, the Light that shines in the darkness and will not be overcome, the pillar of fire by night that led the Israelites out of Egypt, the passion of freedom for faithfulness that gave courage to the pilgrims who endured in New England; in myriad ways and in a rainbow of color like that which came as a sign to Noah, the light of the grace of God speaks to us and calls us on. Imagination is the God-given capacity in each of us to receive the light and allow its illuminating power fullest expression in our hearts, minds, and souls.

CHAPTER 10

Prayer: Correspondence With God

The abscess had penetrated so far that even the Physicians of that day knew that he would not last much longer, and the poor child was terrified for fear her husband would go out of life cursing God and abusing the aid of religion. So she rushed to Catherine and implored her, as she was known to be a giant in prayer, that she would exert herself with God to help the victim. Catherine replied, "The first thing you must know is that at this very moment God is not alienated from him, and therefore cares for him more than it is possible for you or me at our very best to care for him. That is the first thing to realize. And therefore, I cannot ask God to do anything for him that God of the immense loving kindness of His heart would not do, and, as He is God, is therefore doing; but what I will do is that when I go into the Light, I will take him with me."

—Gerald Heard
Ten Questions on Prayer[1]

Prayer comes of a need that springs from deep within us. It is yearning for connection with the indispensable mystery that undergirds life. It is vital to our fullest expression of the persons we are capable of being.

Prayer is important, not as much because of its results as of its experience. Results follow prayers, but the value of prayer cannot be measured by results alone. Prayer is important as a way to correspond, relate to the silent, mysterious, intimate nature of God. To want to make sense of prayer by demonstrating its effects is understandable. But more important than immediate effects, prayer is a way to allow imagination to engage with the power of God that, as we intuitively recognize, dwells at the center of existence.

This intuitive recognition is born out of our need as much as our faith, our ignorance as much as our wisdom, our powerlessness as much as our understanding. We need not apologize for resorting to prayer when we seem to have no other way of changing situations and circumstances under which we suffer. We are constantly led to water when thirsty, food when hungry, another when lonely. Our intuitive movement to God in our powerlessness is similarly appropriate.

The Influence of Prayer

I recall a time when I was a teenager. I had just taken Christianity seriously, having been introduced to Jesus through a conservative youth movement. In the flush of my conversion I prayed that my brother, two years younger than I, would similarly discover Jesus as having meaning for his life. I was amazed and frightened as I saw him, little by little, develop an interest in the things religious about which I prayed for him. I stopped praying for his conversion. I could not agree with my near fundamentalist counselors that he would burn in hell if he did not convert. I was not sure whether my interest in his conversion was for him or for my need to be affirmed. I left it up to him and God. My prayers changed from directing him to caring for him. But the impression continues within me that he was being influenced by my prayers. It broadens my understanding of prayer to acknowledge that I was being influenced by my prayers as well. My brother and I, still in love with one another, have gone our separate ways. Now I remember him, his wife, and their children in my prayers and am connected with them.

I have grown some in wisdom in the years since that episode. I am learning, little by little, to pray that my will will be in harmony with God's rather than the other way around. To pray is to enter consciously and unconsciously into relationship with God. Much happens in that relationship that one cannot anticipate or control. Because it is a mystery, what comes as a result of the relationship is a often a surprise. The one thing that can be said is that praying results in the furtherance of the will of a just and loving God in one's life and in the lives of others.

Why Could We Not?

Do you remember the story in the ninth chapter of the Book of Mark where the disciples' attempt to heal a child of epilepsy was unsuccessful? Jesus came upon the scene and succeeded where their efforts had failed. "Why could we not cast it out?" was their question, and that is our question, too. Why can we not rid ourselves of foolish vanity? Why can we not rid humankind of the demon of self-destruction? Why can we not see others as brothers and sisters, children of God, rather than enemies and strangers? Why can we not see the earth as a source of nourishment to be respected and revered rather than exploited? "Why Lord, could we not rid that boy of that damnable demon?" And Jesus replied, "Only through prayer" (Mark 9:28–29). This kind can come out only through prayer.

In this same episode Jesus encounters the epileptic boy's father. The father had been with the boy for years, caring for him and seeking relief for his affliction. Jesus was one in a long line of sources to which he had appealed for aid. "It dashes him down," explains the father painfully, "and he foams and becomes rigid. It often casts him into the fire and into water to destroy him. Can you do anything?"

Jesus' response is interesting, even puzzling. "If you can!" he says. "All things are possible to those who believe." The father must have been taken aback; the disciples, listening alongside, humbled. The father responds, "If I can, Lord? I do believe. Help thou my unbelief?" Here is a magnificent statement of a condition shared by many of us. We stand on the brink of power to rid ourselves and others of vanity, greed, fear, demons that cast us down. We believe that God can use us for these purposes but we also don't believe it.

"Why can we not?" And Jesus says, "You can." In response to the specific question of the disciples Jesus answers our question as well. "This kind cannot be driven out by anything but prayer." The power we seek is to be found in prayer.

Power and prayer—an unlikely coalition. Much in our secular society teaches us to think of prayer as powerless, a waste of time.

114

If someone's hungry, don't waste your words on prayer. Bake some bread. If you care, don't sit there and pray about it. Get out and do something! But in fact it is we who are powerless. Our bread and actions always fall short, just as did the efforts of the disciples for the epileptic boy's healing.

It is in prayer that the power for action and the appropriate directive for that action will be found. Prayer without action is not sincere. Action without prayer becomes self-serving. Prayer and action are the elements that combine for the power of the resurrecting renewing God of righteousness to find expression through our lives.

Why Prayer?

In the face of awesome forces that oppose us, forces within and around us, we are told that prayer is necessary. Why prayer? Here are three suggestions as to why prayer makes a difference.

1. Prayer Dramatizes Our Basic Condition

Prayer itself, more than the content of the prayer, dramatizes our basic condition. This condition is described by Carl Jung as being "duplex" as opposed to "simplex."[2]

Jung meant that we are not alone in the world. Our true circumstance is not isolation but relationship. Our condition is interdependent, not independent. As soon as we enter prayer, we are addressing life in a manner that assumes relatedness. The courage to risk foolishness by being in prayer, i.e., risking addressing the unknown which might not be there, introduces us to the basic truth of our experience. We are alive in relationship. Martin Buber speaks of this when he tells us that the basic reality of life is meeting. Without meeting there is no reality.

Isolation is an illusion in which each of us has lived and from which many never escape by virtue of circumstances and lack of faith. Jesus says in the words of John of Patmos in the Book of Revelation, "Behold I stand at the door and knock" (Rev. 3:20). Some hear the knocking and open the door. Others assume the noise to be the bothersome rapping of a dead limb blown by an aimless wind in their desert experience.

2. Prayer Opens Our Eyes

Henri Nouwen speaks of this when he says, "It is impressive to see how prayer opens one's eyes. Prayer makes one contemplate and attentive. In place of manipulating, the one who prays stays receptive before the world."[3]

In prayer we are given the perspective by which we can see ourselves and others better illuminated by the light of God's grace, which shines in loving relationship. I have found it helpful at times to pray by speaking one word. It could be one of any number of significant words. I generally use the Hebrew word for God's peace, the peace that passes all understanding, peace that results from the harmony of all parts rather than the sound of only one, *shalom*. I begin by reflecting upon the word and calling definitions to mind, examples of conditions which mean shalom to me. The word then becomes light in my imagination and I hold those I am praying for in the light of shalom. Shalom creates the condition for them that is my prayer.

The light of shalom also directs me by illuminating the individual, situation, or object I hold in the light in such a way that I can better see it, her, or him and gain perspective from the understanding of God's shalom.

3. Prayer Dethrones the Ego

Prayer dethrones our own sense of ourselves as central to the universe. We are tempted to consider ourselves central to compensate for the fearful sense of aloneness that assaults us daily. Our own tendency to what Jung calls a simplex understanding of life is our greatest obstacle to becoming a partner with God in creative and redemptive life work. Pride, which in religious language is also called idolatry, is compensation for our fear of finitude. This fear will plague us, even overwhelm us, if we deny our dependence upon God. Prayer acknowledges our dependence and affirms our relationship with God, easing our aloneness.

Psychology speaks of ego strength as necessary for a "realized" or "actualized person." It is true as far as it goes. In this sense a strong ego is a reflection of a person's understanding and acceptance of self-worth. This awareness is primarily the result of being loved and accepting it. The further and appropriate response of an individual to the recognition of being loved is to love in return. This is a giving of one's self in response to the gift of having been given one's self. The source and flow of love that comes to us in many and varied forms originates in God, and the appropriate recipient of the gift of ourselves, given in response, is God. We are given selfhood that we may give it away. In such a process life continues; dignity, beauty, and truth are affirmed. Pride enthrones the ego and denies our dependence upon the love that comes and affirms our worth. Praying leads us to understand the true source of our worth and encourages our abandon in returning ourselves to the life from which we came. Thomas Merton says this beautifully in *New Seeds of Contemplation:*

> The only true joy on earth is to escape from the prison of our own false self and enter by love into union with the Life who dwells and sings within the essence of every creature and in the core of our own souls. In this love we possess all things and enjoy the fruition of them, finding God in them all. And thus, as we go about the world, everything we meet and everything we see and hear and touch, far from defiling, purifies us and plants in us something more of contemplation and of heaven [4]

Prayer dethrones the ego and puts God in God's rightful place: the center of our lives.

The Beginning of Prayer—Sound Vision

We are nearsighted, every one of us. We'd like to be able to possess the long view—justice, prosperity, security—not just for ourselves but for all peoples. We long to see the realm of God and how to get there, but we cannot see that far. God can and is in the process of taking the creation to that place. But you and I are nearsighted, and that is all the sight we need. We don't have to learn to see better. We have to learn how to use the eyes we have, to stop to look—to look deeply with a sound eye into something, almost anything. A mustard seed, a lost lamb, danger on the road to Jericho, a concerned father, a rebellious son, men and women going through their daily lives—these are parts of the mirror into which we can look to see God and God's way.

Samuel Miller wrote, "Like faith, humility is also the life of the soul, and what is humility but holding common things, and unpretentious people and ordinary events in reverence."[5] To look at what is around us to see all that we can see begins with an attitude of reverent consideration of that upon which we look. Such reverent consideration is prayer. Take time and look. Take time and listen. Take time to understand what is really there. Reverence in this context is time taken to see—a stillness that allows eyes to open, a patience that sees beauty in boots and clouds and rakes and hands and caterpillars. Being reverent, the beginning of prayer, is taking the time to see what we can see.

Martin Buber writes, "He who goes out truly to meet the world goes out, also, to meet God."[6] Going out "truly" to meet the world is not easy. The beginning of prayer is not to reach this state of openness. It is to trust that God is to be found in everyone and everything that the world offers in the cornucopia of experience that constitutes an average day for any of us. The great mystics and religious heroes speak of high moments of such recognition. Learning to see things and people for what they are and valuing them for that is a beginning to being spiritually alive.

Finding Time to Pray

It's one thing to say that looking around is the beginning of prayer. It's much harder to do it. If we are to develop a prayer life, we are going to have to find time to pray. The demands of busy schedules, frenetic recreation, and the loss of hours in front of television sets calls for a discipline of prayer. There is nothing more corrosive of spiritual life in contemporary living than the pace of life that leaves little or no time for silence, meditation, easy and unhurried conversation, contemplation. The words attributed to an anonymous Buddhist monk are instruction for anyone seeking to develop a life of the spirit in our day: *Don't just do something, stand there.*

The story of Thomas Merton's discovery of the power of prayer after facing his powerlessness may speak to you as it does to me. He was a seeker after truth who had disdained religion. That is, until he read Aldous Huxley's novel, *Ends and Means,* which he tells of in his book *The Seven Story Mountain.*[7] "[Huxley] had read widely and deeply and intelligently in all kinds of Christian and oriental mystical literature and had come out with the astounding truth that all of this, far from being a mixture of dreams and magic and charlatanism is very real and serious." In *Pray to Live*, Henri Nouwen says of Merton, "To his alarm, Merton read the conclusion of Huxley that if we want to live differently from wild beasts, we must free the spirit by means of prayer and asceticism."[8]

Prayer and asceticism, prayer and discipline and self-denial. This denial is not to say, "I am nothing, Lord, punish me," but rather, "You are something, God, and I will spend time and energy, I will discipline myself, I will deny myself other involvements so that I may know you."

Nouwen continues: "The word asceticism had up to now only meant a twisting of nature, but Huxley showed Merton that through asceticism the spirit can become itself and find God."[9] Merton shrank from this at this point. We too have shrunk from it, but the message is clear. Prayer is worth working at because it makes a difference.

I and many friends in the church, lay people and clergy, would like very much to have a disciplined life of prayer or meditation but have difficulty conducting our prayer life that way. This is a strange contradiction in our human experience. We have a deep hunger for developing our intuitive capacities, yet our intuitive capacities seem to have no will to organize for their own development. If we are going to find time to pray, we are going to have to structure our lives by the use of our rational ordering capacities.

Spiritual discipline needs to come from within ourselves. We have to genuinely want to find time to pray. Even then it is hard to do because everyday business crowds in. Working with someone else helps, whether a group, a guide, or a fellow seeker. When you are sure that you want to accept a self-disciplined prayer life, be intentional about setting up a system of accountability. It will help immeasurably.

Thinking Toward God

John Baillie, the noted American Baptist writer and preacher, has described prayer as thinking toward God. Earlier we discussed the difficulty of approaching a transcendent reality with rational thought. In *Reality and Prayer*, John McGee said, "God is not an object of thought but our ultimate and intimate concern, the focus of all those ultimate judgments about fact and value which bear intimately on every phase of our existence. In prayer, we come into the presence of One who is over against us yet wholly possessing us, whom we do not know but toward whom all our thoughts inevitably turn."[10]

Here we are confronted with a paradox. Thought, which we give expression to in words, is both incapable of expressing God yet, at the same time, irresistibly attracted to God. How, then, do we correspond? We must ride our rational horse as far as it can take us and then walk as we can into the mystery, supported by our commitment to explore. We cannot abandon rational thought, though we recognize its limitations. It is vital in moving us toward that essential reality that the word *God* means.

A starting point for thinking toward God could be to consider a personal experience of God. It could be a moment of recognition of the wonder of life or the beauty of love. It might be recollection of a time when the screen of the temporal was lifted and the eternal came into view through an experience of music or wilderness or compassion. It may have been literature, some nurture concealed within the written word, that captured an essence of divinity in a time of need or insight. Think back on those times when you have experienced God and begin your prayer there, addressing the reality that touched you in that moment.

I have a friend who envisions God as light. This is scripturally sound and visually effective. He begins his meditation and prayer by visualizing the light of God shining down upon his head and entering the top of his head to illuminate and give his mind inspiration. The starting point is God. As we think toward God, we must think of those symbols and experiences that have had meaning for us in our relationship with the Divine.

Devotional reading has been helpful in beginning prayers. The Psalms can open and reveal depths of understanding of the human condition and God. These can direct thoughts in ways that shape prayers and their response.

I like to think of prayer as correspondence with God. Correspondence means to be in conformity or agreement with one another, to compare closely. It also means written communication, and the essence of both meanings suggests an exchange of thoughts toward the end of mutuality. Writing prayers is an effective discipline in prayer life. In fact, some people find writing the most effective way of self-expression. The advantage of writing is that it uses the linear thought of language and records it for present and later reference. The very act of writing deepens understanding. Often a prayer is answered before the writing of it can be completed.

Writing prayers is just one way to correspond with God. Others dance, some sing. Many of us just open our mouths and talk. Others choose silence. For our purpose we will think of prayer as involving thought, however, so that the meditational practices that encourage the loss of thought toward a oneness with existence are not what we are speaking of here. Thinking toward God is reflection on some aspect of God. It is the light of that reflection that can shine upon all we have to say as we continue the conversation, which is our opening to God.

Being Present in Our Prayers

A young man, not out of his teens, had been killed. It was a tragic accident—sudden, absurd in its loss, one of those situations that could have been avoided, a thousand-to-one chance, nonetheless, the boy was dead. During the memorial service, the boy's father sat in the front row, and, during the time of silent prayer, cried out for all assembled to hear, "God, how can I believe that You are good when you allow my son to be killed? How can I believe in You? My son is dead!" That was a prayer, a deep and real prayer, a statement of his pain and anguish. He was present in his anguished questioning of God. If he was to find God's answer he had to ask the real question. I do not know if he ever heard the answer. I do know that God understands the grief surrounding the death of one's child.

Group activities that encourage honesty and provide compassionate support are a priceless gift to participants. They allow new freedom for many of the participants, a chance to speak of the bitterness, the anger, the frustration, the loneliness, the pain of living. Often they allow participants to express the joy, hope, and happiness of being heard and responded to, of having been given the chance to respond through trust. What was and continues to be appropriate in support group experience is even more appropriate in prayer. We can speak truly to God of our fears, our doubts, our hopes, our anguish, our anxieties, our anger. It is in prayer that we can reach out and, in flights of the imagination, entertain the possibilities of miracles. It is in prayer that we can give expression to the child that dwells in us, as well as the more sophisticated adult. We can talk to God out of our condition.

It may seem strange that it helps to speak to God in prayer about events of our lives. If God is all-knowing, would it not be encroaching upon God with redundancy to parade ourselves before the Divine once again? Yet, my experience is that by speaking words, by articulating my situation, I am granted more clarity and some direction. It is as if it is necessary to speak the words for me to hear the words that God is speaking to me. It is as if God speaks to me as I speak.

Prayer as an End in Itself

There is a growing integration of spiritual, physical, and intellectual awareness and activity resulting from the discipline of the practice of prayer. As in the experience of teenage telephone conversations with loved ones, content is secondary, relationship is primary. The effect upon daily life is integrative and life-affirming. Very little has been said here of petition in prayer, of asking for things. This is not because such asking is inappropriate. We are invited, encouraged in scripture and in the teaching of the spiritually enlightened, to bring all aspects of our lives to God in prayer. Bring our dreams, concerns, and needs as we know them. "Ask and it will be given," is Jesus' counsel. The basic value of prayer, however, is its function as an experience of relationship with God. Thus it is more an end than a means. The practice of prayer is at least as significant as the content of the prayers.

The practice of prayer encourages righteousness. Righteousness is one of those revered biblical words that most people today would be hard pressed to define. Yet it is a condition that is sorely needed in all times, none more so than our time in western civilization. Righteousness means right relationship, right relationship with God by those in covenant with God. Prayer is intentional relationship with God and as such is an end in itself. Justice, mercy, loving kindness, wisdom, and humility spring from right relationship with God. Prayers of talking to and listening to God, prayers in words and silence, prayers of honest expression of one's self, one's dreams, one's fears and feelings, prayers of open receptivity to God's reply, all prayers are first and foremost seeking right relationship with God and through God. First and foremost in God's will and reply is right relationship with those who pray. In this essential sense prayers are ends in themselves. The ills of our society, ourselves, and our earth are essentially ills of wrong relationship. We turn to God as the disciples turned to Jesus after he had healed the sick child whom their efforts had not affected. "Why could we not cast out the demon?" they asked. "Only through prayer," answered Jesus. Healing is found in right relationship.

CHAPTER 11

Dreams: A Voice of Self and God

Tom's dreams led him into the only way he could follow
to regain his health. They led him like a thread from the
labyrinth of his own thoughts to renewed healthy attitudes, to a free conscience, and to reconstructed relationships. We may therefore assume an intelligence
within his psyche, responsible for these meaningful
dreams. For reasons which will appear more clearly as
we go on, I do not hesitate to call this intelligence
"God". God is the name men give to the purposeful, lu-
minous power which crosses our lives; our dreams are
one of the manifestations of this power.

—John A. Sanford
Dreams: God's Forgotten Language[1]

Dreams are a voice of self and God that come as gifts to give life to
our days and direction to our actions. This is true of all dreams,
whether daydreams, night dreams, dreams of better days, dreams
of better ways. They hold aspects of ourselves and confront us
with a reality we have not yet realized or integrated into our
consciousness.

With our conditioned mistrust of the ambiguous and the intuitive, dreams often seem like clouds and lace linings, distrac-
tions from reality, the preoccupation of wasted lives. But Langston
Hughes is right. Lives without dreams are like broken-winged
birds condemned to an element that is part of their reality but not
the part for which their unique soaring spirits long.

Hold fast to dreams
for when dreams die
life is a broken winged bird
that cannot fly.
Hold fast to dreams
for when dreams go
life is a frozen field
covered with snow.[2]

Lives without dreams are like barren fields—frozen and life-less. Dreams are part of the spiritual gift that we are given to draw us toward wholeness, whole persons, and a whole society.

Dreams—A Psychological Perspective

For Freud, dreams were significant revelations of the chaotic activity of the unconscious which, once analyzed, could be used to combat the unconscious energies by bringing their efforts to the light of conscious awareness and subsequent willful control. One of his promising students to whom he had looked to assume a major part in the continuation of his school of thought, Carl Jung, differed with Freud at just this significant point. Jung believed that the unconscious was an energy source for wholeness rather than disintegration. Consciousness was important, and human will had its prominent place in Jung's view, but the unconscious was neither opposed to nor intent upon subverting the accomplishments of the conscious. Just the opposite. For Jung the unconscious is rich in personal insight and is connected with a collective resource beyond individual experience. It speaks in symbol and image to call a consciousness to awareness of ignored potentialities that are necessary for growth and movement toward wholeness or as Jung called it, individuation. Jung wrote of the unconscious,

> We, therefore, emphatically affirm that in addition to repressed material the unconscious contains all the psychic components that have fallen below the threshold as well as subliminal sense perceptions. Moreover, we know from abundant experience as well as for theoretical reasons that the unconscious also contains all the material that has not yet reached the threshold of consciousness. These are

the seeds of future conscious contents. Equally, we have reason to suppose that the unconscious is never quiescent in the sense of being inactive but is ceaselessly engaged in grouping and regrouping contents. This activity should be thought of as completely autonomous only in pathological cases. Normally, it is co-ordinated with the conscious mind in a compensatory relationship.[3]

Freud and Jung agreed that there is power in the unconscious that is capable of overwhelming an individual. They both recognized instinctual energies and shadow dimensions within us that, when repressed, result in their being energized for disintegrative purposes. Freud believed that the hope for surviving these energies rests with the consciousness of the individual person. Jung believed that a guide for integration exists within the psyche or soul. For Jung, consciousness plays its part but as a partner with the unconscious. The power is to be respected but not feared.

My understanding of dreams is largely dependent upon Jungian thought. It is my view that dreams are not demonic or amoral but are in large degree expressions of a desire for our personal reconciliation with our own alienated parts, vulnerabilities, and strengths. This reconciliation is toward the end of our integrated being, which is experienced as freedom to be who we are in relationship with all and each.

Jung suggested that religion plays a unique role in integrating the conscious and unconscious. Religion embraces the ability to listen to and believe in the message of symbols.

> There must be a union of the two parts [conscious and unconscious] for failing that there is no doubt how the matter would be decided. The primitive man could inevitably lapse back into repression. But that union is possible only where still valid and therefore living religion exists which allows the primitive man adequate means of expression through a richly developed symbolism. In other words, in his dogmas and rites this religion must possess a mode of thinking and acting that harks back to the most primitive level.[4]

It needs to be understood that "primitive" does not mean undeveloped or ignorant in Jung's thought. The primitive is basic life force. "Civilized" humanity, in Jung's view, is losing touch with its life-sustaining origins, with its primitive source. We do not need to give up the knowledge and refinements civilization provides us, but we do need to integrate it with our primitive vitality.

Using Jung's word, repressing the primitive would result in cruel unconscious projections and violent rejections of parts of us recognized in others, unclaimed as our own, yet vital for our full humanity's realization. Religion is the primary integrator of our essential, i.e., primitive, vitality and our civilized accommodations. Dreams are a way that God reminds us of all aspects of ourselves and invites us to accept responsibility for and rejoice in our whole condition. It is an essential aspect of God's grace that those parts of ourselves of which we are most afraid can be accepted and incorporated into our wholeness for God's purposes and our happiness. Understanding that God loves all of who we are calls us to accept all of who we are and to find, through contemplation, confession and forgiveness, ways to meet our needs short of destructive action, conscious or unconscious.

The Language of Dreams

Dreams communicate by engaging the dreamer with an image. They flow with a fluidity that makes time, space, and content secondary to the message they contain. Their message is to be found in the dreamer's dynamic relationship with the dream. Your dream may be similar to mine, but that does not mean they are similar in their meanings for us individually.

There are symbols that appear to be universal in the language of dreams. Carl Jung referred to them as archetypes. But the archetypes are flexible and never literal nor single in their meaning. The dreamer is the final authority regarding the meaning of the dream content.

Extensive lists of possible meanings of symbols and images can be found interpreting shapes, colors, subject matter. Dream symbols do have content for our understanding but the possible meanings are many. The dreamer must interact with the symbols for them to find their meanings. It may well be that the dream symbols have something or nothing to do with meanings found on someone's list of the meanings of symbols. The central fact to keep in mind is that the dreamer is the authority who determines meaning. Suggested meanings from a list or another's comments can stimulate the dreamer's imagination, but the meaning of the dream image is already resident in the dreamer's mind waiting to be given room for its fuller expression in consciousness.

Are All Dreams Religious?

I, for one, find great difficulty in separating experience into religious and nonreligious categories. There is a true sense in which "every common bush is afire with God," to quote Elizabeth Barrett Browning.[5] It would be consistent to say then that every dream, every person, every experience is lit in some degree by the divine light. By virtue of predisposition, ill temper, fatigue, narrowness, self-righteousness, bigotry, whatever, there are those meetings where I do not perceive the "thou", the divine light of the other. Those are not religious experiences. When I engage the other as "thou" it is a religious experience. What this boils down to is that all experiences, bushes and dreams included, are potentially religious if we are prepared in faith to see the sacred light that shines in them. When we fail to see that light the experience is mundane. Ann and Barry Ulanov offer the following description regarding religious experience:

> the encounter with original mystery, with God, with the primary event . . . not only gives us being but re-creates us throughout our lives. . . . We fall away sometimes, committing perjury against the truth of the encounter of the human and the divine, perhaps even denying that it has happened at all. Religion explores and reenacts our journey back to the primordial experience that binds us to itself, describing that journey as a passage toward the light, that finally the inscrutable and evanescent presence of the extra-ordinary shines through the most ordinary daily occurrences.[6]

All dreams come with light. Few of us are ready, consciously, to take advantage of the light to see what is revealed. It has been shown that a cathartic function is served by the very act of dreaming that doesn't involve conscious work with dreams. However, a clear impression that dreams give is that they wish to be recognized by our consciousness, that they have messages, perspectives that we should acknowledge.

All dreams are not understood as religious because we do not recognize the light or realize the potential for unity of self and God that they offer. But when we see the light and realize the unity offered, what Jung called the compensatory function, we grow toward wholeness and feel awe before the source of these revelations that encourage our becoming.

Listening to Our Dreams

Before moving into a discussion of engaging dreams I want to emphasize again that you, the dreamer, are the authority regarding the meaning of your dreams. Someone else can be of help in encouraging and stimulating engagement, but you are the one for whom the message is intended. The importance of what is there to be found is known within you.

In order to listen to dreams we need to develop a system of recording them. Dreams have the habit of seeping through the cracks of consciousness and disappearing below consciousness into the realm of their origins. Keeping a dream log is a way of keeping track of the messages that come in dream form.

Dreams often occur in sequence and have relationship to previous and future dreams. A log gives you opportunity for this perspective. Jung says of this:

> It rarely occurs that dreams are either exclusively positive or exclusively negative. As a rule one finds both aspects but usually one is stronger than the other. . . . If our dream were the only one we possess we could hardly hope to unlock its innermost meaning, but we have quite a number of dreams in series. . . . I never, if I can help it, interpret one dream by itself. As a rule, a dream belongs in a series. There is a continuity in consciousness despite the fact that it is regularly interrupted by sleep. There is probably a continuity of unconscious process and perhaps even more so than with the events of consciousness. In any case, my experience is in favor of the probability that dreams are the visible links in a chain of unconscious events.[']

A log can be any pad or notebook set near your bed for recording your dreams as soon as possible after having dreamt them. Whether during the night or in the morning, writing the dream in detail not only records it but deepens, and in some ways, continues it. You need not write the entire dream in the middle of the night. A few key words will prompt recall in the morning.

The discipline of recording is important. The more we are tuned into our dreams and take time to record them, bring them into consciousness, the more our awareness of dreams develops. Electroencephalogram monitoring during sleep has shown that all persons monitored dream, whether they remember it or not.

One need not remember an entire dream to gain from it. A fragment is helpful and frequently surprisingly insightful. Collecting dream fragments serves to prime the pump of awareness and leads to greater recall as one works at it.

A dream group encourages discipline in recording dreams and in stimulating understanding. If it is to be ongoing it is better to keep a dream group small—five members or less—otherwise the material to be dealt with outstrips the time and energy of the group. The group agrees to keep dream logs and meet regularly (weekly works well) to discuss their dreams.

An approach to dream understanding that considers all symbols in the dream to be laden with meaning is helpful. It is understood that every person and every object in a dream is the creation of the dreamer's dream source. As such each is best understood from the perspective of the dreamer. If one dreams of being in a prison with another person, for example, and is aware of a rose growing in the middle of the exercise yard, consider, even act out each symbol and role the dream presents. This content is from a dream of mine. In a dream group I described and spoke for the various parts in the dream, commenting on the sequence and my feelings through it. First I was myself and then became the other prisoner, and African American. I then spoke as the prison and explained why I, as the prison building, was the shape I was. I also was the rose and recognized beauty and promise in the midst of my imprisonment. Throughout my dream work the group members listened carefully and asked clarifying questions to be sure they understood what I was saying. This helped refine my own clarity as I regularly referred to the dream as resource in order to confirm or deny the group-suggested meanings. I was led far beyond the level of understanding I had when I first recorded the dream.

The simple process of reading your recorded dreams out loud provides insight. Verbalization allows reflection that silent reading seems less able to provide. In a religious community, one is aided by a reverent appreciation of the source of dreams and respect for each member of the group as a beloved child of God. Prayer used in a dream group focuses the members upon God, the dream source, and encourages the expression of a reverent spirit that is helpful in any relationship of persons as well as respectful use of the dreams themselves. In our secular culture dreams are seldom publicly considered an important resource for individual and group development and direction. More intuitive cultures have long regarded dreams as important. When my friend Terry Gibson and I made arrangements to see the Sioux medicine man, Ellis Chips, his one question to Terry on the phone, when deciding whether to see us, was, "Do you believe in dreams?" Terry, an ordained Methodist minister, who wrote his Ph.D. dissertation on archetypal aspects of Jungian psychology, answered "Yes!" without hesitation.

John Neihardt records the dream that became the power vision of a Sioux medicine man in his book, *Black Elk Speaks*.[8] He tells how the entire tribe came to act out the vision so that its power could be released to Black Elk and, through him, to the tribe.

When Black Elk was nine years old, he was struck down with pains in his legs and couldn't walk. Feverish and immobile, in the midst of disease, a vision came to him. First he saw two Indians flying at him like arrows coming out of the sky. They came with flaming spears and took him with them through the air to another place. "We three were there alone in the middle of a great white plain with snowy hills and mountains staring at us and it was very still but there were whispers," he said. "Then the two men spoke together and they said, 'Behold him, the being with four legs.' I looked and saw a bay horse standing there and he began to speak, 'Behold me,' he said, 'my life history you shall see.' Then he wheeled about to where the sun goes down and said, 'Behold them, their history you shall know.' I looked and there were twelve dark horses yonder all abreast with necklaces of bison hooves and they were beautiful. But I was frightened because their manes were lightning and their nostrils were thunder." The dream continued with decorated animals of the plains coming from the four points of the compass. There were geese flying and a great rainbow tepee where he met his six grandfathers.

Suppose a young man today were to come from a fever and coma to announce that he had had a dream such as this. The symbols would probably be contemporary and out of his experience. What would we do? How would we handle it? Likely as not, if it persisted and he persisted in telling us about it, we would find a psychiatrist in whom we trusted and send him there. We might well find some way to categorize him within the limits of our understanding and the vision would wither. He would be taught that imagination, vision, is to be held down and kept private. For lack of expression the vision would atrophy.

What would have happened to Isaiah as he stood in the temple of God and beheld the beauty of seraphim and the train of God that filled the temple? What of the glowing coal that came down to purge his guilt-filled lips and open his ears to the voice that said, "Whom shall I send? Who will go for me?" What would we do with Joel who speaks of visions and the possibilities of men and women, young and old, the people of God who will dream dreams and see visions—those who will dare call upon the name of the Lord? And our community, how many visions, inspirations, dreams, grand possibilities have we nipped in the bud because of our fear of others' rejections or our own confusion about the language or worth of dreams?

Black Elk was pursued by his dream for nine years. In a culture that encouraged expression of the supernatural, he could not find courage to give it expression until he was eighteen. It persisted within him with such power that he knew he would die if he didn't tell it, so he found his way to a medicine man who heard his story. The tribe responded by acting out Black Elk's vision. They gathered thirty-six horses and painted them, put elk's teeth around some and portrayed light and radiance on others. Black Elk was put in the middle. A great tepee was painted as a rainbow, and six men portraying the grandfathers were put into it. Black Elk, in the center of the drama, acted out his dream. The tribe participated as well. Through his dream and the community's faith he was empowered. That power became the incentive that moved him into his calling to become a man of healing. He was with his people as their medicine man through Custer's last stand, through the massacre at Wounded Knee and the violation of subsequent treaties. He was with his people in their humiliation and served them as healer and visionary. He was life-giving for them because his vision was given life by the tribe.

Black Elk's vision was extraordinary. Many of our dreams will be less powerful than that great vision, but every dream brings light and power. Some dreams will stand out as significant beyond the others, challenging us to engage them and engage life. Dreams recognized and engaged give life.

The Shadow Coming to Life

Carl Jung wrote that "Everyone carries a shadow and the less it is recognized in an individual's conscious life, the blacker and more dense it is. If an inferiority is conscious, one always has a chance to correct it. . . . But if it is repressed and isolated from consciousness, it never gets corrected." He then concludes that if the shadow is never brought to consciousness, "In all events, it forms an unconscious nag." Dreams are understood to be vehicles for, among other things, the shadow's nagging. Another way to speak of this is that God is continually calling us to be reconciled with our true condition of vulnerability, what Jung calls our "inferior childish or primitive qualities which in a way vitalize and embellish human existence."[9] This is a gentle definition for drives within us of which we are much afraid. Jung suggests that the density of the danger is increased by our repeatedly repressing the fear, the shadow. There is sin in not trusting in the grace of God, who calls us to confess, to present our incomplete selves before the Divine One and trust in God's grace for forgiveness and recreation. But sin is more yet. It is the acts of destruction that result from our projections, our refusal to accept responsibility for our incompleteness, and overreaction to the incompleteness of others. Laurens van de Post, a student of Jung's and man of the spirit in his own right recalls Jung's thoughts:

> I clearly remember him saying to me that the individual who withdraws his shadow from his neighbor and finds it in himself and is reconciled to it as to an estranged brother is doing a task of great universal importance. He added that the future of mankind depended on the speed and extent to which individuals learnt to withdraw their shadows from others and reintegrate them honorably within themselves.[10]

Dreams call our shadows to the light of God's grace and work for our reconciliation with God, neighbor, and self. It is the dream of Grace that we know the wholeness of such reconciliation. God is ever at work in various ways, none more so than in the Christ Spirit that was and is in Jesus, reconciling the world to the God self. In that reconciliation we will know the fullness and freedom of life, find reason for humility and the basis for true compassion and justice action.

I am convinced that in our waking and sleeping God calls us to fuller and freer existence by grace for purposes of justice and joy. Learning to listen to and interact with our dreams—night dreams, daydreams, holding fast to our dreams as Langston Hughes gives us counsel—will facilitate our movement in the direction God would have us go, which is our wholeness and God's joy.

CHAPTER 12

The Mystical Experience: Opened By Grace, Called to Serve

> And now we are saved absolutely, we need not say from what, we are at home in the universe, and, in principle and in the main, feeble and timid creatures as we are, there is nothing within the world or without it that can make us afraid.
>
> —Bernard Bosanquet[1]

There is an experience of awareness called mystical insight. In this state one discovers an undifferentiated unity, a oneness, pure consciousness. It is an encounter with the One in whom all things are one. Though it may be sought with all discipline and determination it seems to come of its own accord. It comes to some who diligently seek it. It comes to others from out of the blue with no seeming preparation or expectation. It is clear that those who search for it with dedication can find it. It is clear as well that mystical awareness breaks into all of our lives in some form or another, whether sought or not. It is the touch of God, a breakthrough of grace. It may be a fleeting touch that leaves one grateful for the exposure to a higher joy and hoping for more, vaguely discontent with what heretofore passed as meaning. Or it may have been an experience of such power that life will never be the same. There is no doubt that one has been graced with a knowing of Truth that is akin to being allowed into the mind and heart of God. There will be "dark nights of the soul" but when the clouds break, when we crash out of the woods in which all bearings were lost, the Truth of the grace previously encountered continues.

Experiences of this kind, experiences of beauty and love and union, are connections of one's soul with the Soul of creation. Experiences such as this come to us in varying degrees throughout our lives. There are those who, for whatever reason, believe in grace at the center of existence and are more apt to receive the gifts of grace when they come. Others ignore or shrug off the life-expanding and affirming moments. Perhaps it is because we have been conditioned to be uncomfortable with silence, with waiting. Perhaps we believe that our lives are not worthwhile unless they are full of producing or consuming. Perhaps we have been touched but know no one with whom to speak of the experience; thus it passes unnamed and fades from consciousness. Still experiences happen.

Thomas Merton poetically and perceptively speaks of the steady onslaught of seeds of grace that could take root in our souls:

> Every moment and every event of everyone's life on earth plants something in our soul. For just as the wind carries thousands of winged seeds, so each moment brings with it germs of spiritual vitality that come to rest imperceptibly in the minds and wills of individuals. Most of these unnumbered seeds perish and are lost, because we are not prepared to receive them: for such seeds as these cannot spring up anywhere except in the good soil of freedom, spontaneity and love.[2]

You ask yourself if you have had such moments. Yes! Yes, you have. They are the moments of connection and belonging, of loving and being loved, of seeing, hearing, and thrilling. Music can take us to the threshold of mystical awareness and on occasion across it. The arts in their many forms, when they accurately reflect us or reveal reality in a new guise, set recognition in motion that allows us transcendence from mundane conditions. From that perspective we near the spiritual insight of our shared identity with others. Recognizing this, the love of God can break in upon us, grant us union with the lost, the broken, the outcast. We are then moved to compassion and service so that the beauty and interdependence of all lives and life will not be denied or ignored but honored and defended.

There are other moments: moments of beauty, beauty that crushes our souls but does not bruise them; the moment of see-

136

ing, as if for the first time really seeing, one's child or grandchild, any child; the recognition of life continuing through seasons, through calamity, greater than death, day in, day out. On and on we are brought near the experience of identity with and reverence for all life, all existence. Every person, every object is a sacred vessel in which we can perceive eternity and the Eternal One if we can learn to patiently revere.

There are moments in our lives when we know reverence and see God, recognized or not. In these moments we are in the essence of love, the heart of God. Here we also know the essence of Jesus. Our experience of the grace which dwells at the center of existence and permeates all of existence opens our imagination to the Spirit of Christ that moved, moves in the life of Jesus. He no longer is just a cardboard cut-out to be set alongside a Sunday school diorama, a plastic or ceramic infant to be placed in a creche at Christmas. He no longer is vague and sentimental, nor is he any longer in possession of the mean literalists who use him to manipulate you into affirming their polemic. He is alive and fleshed out, a lover of life, a dancer of dances, an embracer of people, particularly people who are overlooked by others, whose beauty has been missed. He is a teller of stories that open to show us ourselves and God. He is a man of passion who cries with the prophets over the blindness of the people who have been entrusted by grace to honor holiness yet ignore injustice. He cries for those who suffer; he cries for those lost ones who do not know they are lost, those who are so often the cause of others' suffering. He is the embodiment of God's love, the incarnation of grace encountered at the center of all being and beings, the soul of existence. At that center we find our souls' centers and fullest life.

Characteristics of the Mystical Experience

By reviewing and analyzing accounts of mystical experiences, scholars have brought reason to bear in an effort to understand and tell others of the nature of the experience. Reading these lists is not unlike being asked to understand what it is to be in love by measuring vital signs. The following list is a summary that I believe calls attention to the most frequently mentioned characteristics of a mystical experience. They are vital signs of a unity that when listed become distorted. Still, linear thought is a gift of God as well as holistic mentation. It can be the line that leads to knowing God.

1. Ineffability—beyond rational categories
2. Noetic—One author writes, "They result in insight into depths of truth unplumbed by the discursive intellect, insights which carry with them a tremendous sense of authority"[3]
3. Transiency—they often happen in a few moments, hardly ever more than minutes, and pass, leaving deep impressions
4. Union—a consciousness of the oneness of all things
5. Timelessness—in an eternal nonsequential now

Your religious experiences, your moments of reverence, your being moved by the sacred, your mystical insights all are valid whether they provided you with one or five of the characteristics on the list. It is definitely not the intention of this list that an orthodoxy of religious experience be encouraged. The apostle Paul struggled with this in his churches as he attempted to affirm the gifts of the Spirit while calling attention to the undergirding reality of God, which is love, a love against which all gifts of the Spirit must be measured. Know that the experience of the love of God is the central experience of the Christian. But also know that opening to that love with your whole mind, heart, and soul can bring you to a union with God in love that results in insight into depths of truth unplumbed by objective analysis.

Stories of the Mystical Experience

The following are stories told by those to whom experiences happened. They are not doctrinally orthodox, attributing power and grace to one religious dogma or another. They are not self-consciously Christian, but the truth they reveal is fully consistent with the truth of Jesus. All the storytellers have some connection with the Christian faith as their basic spiritual orientation, but each story is more than a testimony to the truth of the faith. Each account is extremely personal and evolves from the context of each person's whole life. The truth they find is not only consistent with their faith but informs it. The stories are told to add definition to the word *mystical* and to encourage understanding of your own experience.

My Own Story

A member of one of my congregations had spent her teenage years as a German citizen during Hitler's rise and reign of power. Her father was a Nazi official of some middle rank and she, out of loyalty to father and fatherland, was not confronted with the darkness of her time until after the war. The shock to her foundations was violent, and her life vibrates yet with pain and resulting uncertainty. Out of our conversations I was giving serious consideration to the reality of the brutal in God and in human experience. It was these thoughts that rolled across my unconscious and conscious mind as I worked my way that summer across wilderness trails in the Sierra Nevada of central California, accompanied by two friends and my son, moving to high altitude lakes and peaks for a few days of fishing, climbing, and grandeur. In two days we had found a high country campsite and settled in for daily excursions. The first evening, following dinner, I took myself apart from the others and climbed a near ridge as the sun set. There, surrounded by primitive and profound beauty, I pondered the power of the earth, its constant heaves and thrusts, its tearing down and building up, its seeming impersonal brutality. Standing there I found myself taken over by a sense of presence that was not as if another was there but as if I had opened to a presence that was everywhere, yet with me personally. As the setting sun reflected upon the steep slopes and ridges of glaciated granite I recognized an answer to the question that I had been groping with about God's brutality and life's capacity to destroy. I later attempted to capture that understanding with a poem. I stayed on the ridge for awhile but lost an accurate sense of time. It was a state of being out of myself yet at the same time within my body. I walked quietly to and fro feeling elevated, yet my feet were on the ground. I was filled with the experience of presence that unified the brutal and the tender, life and death, all of creation and me. I would have liked to remain in that state but knew I could not; slowly, still feeling the joy of connection, I worked my way back to the campsite. I tried to tell the others of the experience but was not able to do it with anything that approached shared experience.

The closest that I came to sharing this most powerful of mystical insights was when I read the poem later in the year as part of a memorial service for a young man of my parish who died tragically. Loved ones seemed to hear in the words what I had found on that Sierra ridge.

Rising as some stone hand thrust,
    with jagged fingers extended,
Into the thin atmosphere of 12,000 feet,
It stands and endures
    the winters and springs of life
    as it can.
There is little apparent gentleness
    in the force of freeze and thaw
    that sends the great stones
    down to pulverize themselves
    and what else they may impact
    on their rapid but brief flight,
    their careening way,
    to the base of their mother cliff.
And always, pulling, pressing, chiseling
    the wind and the water work their slow
    steady way to wear down the mighty
    mountain.
Ruthless destruction? Incessant decay?
Yes, but more.
Process of life with movement leaving room
    for yet other life
    to grow from the gravel and the dust.
Richer for the movement into new form
    of the previous stone,
    the new soil welcomes seed,
    and a sprout, a new green thought,
    tender yet persistent,
    finds the morning sun
    as the shadow of the mountain slowly
    passes with the turning of the earth.

Margaret Isherwood

The following is repeated by F. C. Happold in his book, *Mysticism: A Study and An Anthology,* in the chapter titled "Prologue: The Timeless Moment." It is the story told by Margaret Isherwood in her book, *The Root of the Matter* (Gollancz) of an experience she had when she was nine.

> Suddenly the Thing happened, and as everybody knows, it cannot be described in words. The Bible phrase, "I saw the heavens open," seems as good as any if not taken literally. I remember saying to myself, in awe and rapture, "So it's like this; now I know what Heaven is like, now I know what they mean in church." The words of the 23rd Psalm came into my head and I began repeating them: "He maketh me to lie down in green pastures; He leadeth me beside the still waters." Soon it faded and I was alone in the meadow with the baby and the brook and the sweet-smelling lime trees. But though it passed and only the earthly beauty remained, I was filled with great gladness. I had seen the "far distances."[4]

Winifred Holtby

At the age of thirty-three, while at the height of her power as a novelist, Winifred Holtby was told by a specialist that she might not have more than two years to live. Compelled by bodily weakness to give up her work, her whole being in rebellion, she was one day, feeling very tired and dispirited, walking up a hill and came to a trough outside a farmhouse. Its surface was frozen over and some lambs were gathered round it.

She broke the ice for them with her stick, and as she did so heard a voice within her saying, "Having nothing, yet possessing all things." It was so distinct that she looked around startled, but she was alone with the lambs on the top of the hill. Suddenly, in a flash, the grief, the bitterness, the sense of frustration disappeared; all desire to possess power and glory for herself vanished away, and never came back. . . . The moment of "conversion" on the hill of Monks Risborough, she said with tears in her eyes, was the supreme spiritual experience of her life. She always associated it afterwards with the word of Bernard Bosanquet on Salvation:

"And now we are saved absolutely, we need not say from what, we are at home in the universe, and, in principle and in the main, feeble and timid creatures as we are, there is nothing within the world or without it that can make us afraid."[5]

Dr. R. M. Bucke

William James wrote of many religious experiences. He tells of the mystical experience of Dr. R. M. Bucke.

I had spent the evening in a great city, with two friends reading and discussing poetry and philosophy. We parted at midnight. I had a long drive to my lodgings. My mind, deeply under the influence of the ideas, images, and emotions called up by the reading and talk was calm and peaceful. I was in a state of quiet, even passive enjoyment, as it were, through my mind. All at once, without warning of any kind, I found myself wrapped in a flame-colored cloud. For an instance I thought of fire, an immense conflagration somewhere close by in that great city; the next instant I knew that that fire was in myself. Directly afterwards there came upon me a sense of exultation, of immense joyousness, accompanied or immediately followed by an intellectual illumination quite impossible to describe. Among other things, I did not merely come to believe, I saw the universe is not composed of dead matter, but it, on the contrary, is a living Presence; I became conscious in myself of eternal life. It was not a conviction that I would have eternal life, but a consciousness that I possessed eternal life then; I saw that all men are immortal; that the cosmic order is such that without any peradventure all things worked together for the good of each and all; that the foundation principle of the world, of all the worlds, is what we call love, and that the happiness of each and all is in the long run certain. The vision lasted a few seconds and was gone; but the memory of it and the sense of reality of it has remained during the quarter century which has since elapsed. I knew that what the vision showed was true. I had attained to a point of view that conviction, I may say consciousness, has never, even during periods of the deepest depression, been lost.[6]

Simone Weil

In *Waiting For God,*[7] twentieth-century saint Simone Weil's account of dissatisfaction and faithful waiting with the church, she tells us of her enlightenment and the posture she took toward the church because of it. The spiritual autobiography of this talented woman, born in Paris in 1909 and known for her philosophical genius and rare powers of thought, is contained in the long letter which she wrote to her friend, the Dominican Father Perrin, before leaving France in 1942, a little over a year before her death in England. It is a spiritual autobiography of peculiar interest for our times. In it she tells how, as an adolescent, though remaining with the Christian inspiration, she saw the problem of God as one insoluble for the human mind. She decided to leave it alone, neither affirming nor denying anything. She avoided prayer since she feared its power of suggestion; she desired above all to keep her intellectual integrity.

In 1938 she spent ten days, from Palm Sunday to Easter Tuesday, at Sol mes, following, in spite of the violent headaches to which she was subject, all the liturgical services. There she met an English Catholic, who introduced her to the English metaphysical poets of the seventeenth century. Thus she came in contact with George Herbert's poem "Love," which she learned by heart and used to recite to herself.

It was during one of these recitations that, as I told you, Christ himself came down and took possession of me.

In my arguments about the insolubility of the problem of God I had never seen the possibility of that, a real contact, a person to person, here below, between a human being and God. I had vaguely heard tell of things of this kind, but I had never believed in them. In the "Fioretti" the accounts of apparitions rather put me off if anything, like the miracles in the Gospels. Moreover, in this sudden possession of me by Christ, neither my senses nor my imagination had any part; I only felt in the midst of my suffering the presence of love, like that which one can read in the smile of a beloved face. . . . God in his mercy had prevented me from reading the mystics, so that it should be evident to me that I had not invented this absolutely unexpected contact.

Yet I still half refused, not my love but my intelligence. For it seemed to me certain, and I still think so today, that one cannot wrestle enough with God if one does it out of pure regard for truth. Christ likes us to prefer truth to him because, being Christ, he is truth. If one turns aside from him to go towards truth, one will not go far before falling into his arms.[8]

To some an experience of this sort comes only once in a lifetime. With Simone Weil it was not isolated. She used to say the "Our Father" in Greek every morning with absolute attention and often while she was working in the vineyard.

At times the very first words tear my thoughts from my body and transport it to a place outside space where there is neither perspective nor point of view. The infinity of the ordinary expanses of perception is replaced by an infinity to the second or sometimes the third degree. At the same time, filling every part of this infinity of infinity, there is a silence, a silence which is not an absence of sound but which is the object of a positive sensation, more positive than that of sound. Noises, if there are any, only reach me after crossing the silence.

Sometimes, also, during this recitation or at other moments, Christ is present with me in person, but his presence is infinitely more real, more moving, more clear than on the first occasion he took possession of me.[9]

Simone Weil had become a true mystic. Those who read her story may say that she had become a saint. Yet, and this is her particular interest for our time, she refused to be baptized into the church she loved. In her letter to Father Perrin she gives her reasons. For her, Plato was a mystic, Dionysus and Osiris in a certain sense Christ himself, the Bhagavad Gita, a revelation of God. Christianity, she felt, was catholic by right but not in fact, not a truly incarnated Christianity; too much was outside it.

Having so intense and painful a sense of this urgency, I should betray the truth, that is to say the aspect of truth which I see, if I left the point, were I have been since my birth, at the intersection of Christianity and everything that is not Christian.[10]

St. Augustine

The great mystics of the past have written much for our perusal but little of what they wrote tells of their personal enlightenment. They wrote to teach and guide their listeners and readers to individual experience of the "touch of God."

St. Augustine was born in A.D. 354 and died in A.D. 430. The following account comes from Book VII of his famous confessions.

Being admonished by all this to return to myself, I entered into my own depths, with You as guide; and I was able to do it because You were my helper. I entered, and with the eye of my soul, such as it was, I saw Your unchangeable Light shining over that same eye of my soul, over my mind. It was not the light of everyday that the eye of flesh can see, nor some greater light of the same order, such as might be if the brightness of our daily light should be seen shining with a more intense brightness and filling all things wih its greatness. Your light was not that, but other, altogether other than all

144

such lights. Nor was it above my mind as oil above the water it floats on, nor as the sky is above the earth; it was above because it made me, and I was below because made by it. He who knows the truth knows that Light, and he that knows the Light knows eternity. Charity knows it. O eternal truth and true love and beloved eternity! Thou art my God, I sigh to Thee by day and night. When first I knew Thee, Thou didst lift me up so that I might see that there was something to see, but that I was not yet the man to see it. And Thou didst beat back the weakness of my gaze blazing upon me too strongly, and I was shaken with love and with dread. And I knew that I was far from Thee in the region of unlikeness, as if I heard Thy voice from on high: "I am the food of grown men: grow and you shall eat Me. and you shall not change Me into yourself as bodily food but into Me you shall be changed."[11]

So? If hints of mystical union abound on all sides but one does not see them as such it is likely that one has been trained to ignore them, to look elsewhere for landmarks in life's journey. Even then they break through. What then? Ignore and deny again? I suppose it is possible but I doubt if we can ever forget the moment, the moments when we were touched by God's grace. It is possible to name it in some other way, for example, use a road sign that points away from God, away from the center of reality where the Christ Spirit, the Word dwells. The naming is a faith decision no matter what name we choose. I believe a correct name for that which is beyond naming is God, the One in whom all things are one, the One in whom all persons find their life and meaning in just and compassionate relationship ordered by grace. And the correct name is Jesus Christ in whom God's Holy Spirit finds full human expression. And the name is your name and mine, by the grace of God. But only in that we are made one in the mystical union by the One whose face is found in beauty, whose will is expressed in love, whose dream is revealed in justice.

We, who follow that dream, we, who open to and pray to give expression in our living to that love, we, who are blessed to behold that beauty, we are called by God, who speaks out of the center of reality, to faithfulness, which is servant living in the way of Jesus. For those with religious genius such as Simone Weil, faithfulness to God and the people of God may mean living outside the community of faith for the life of the faith community. For the rest of us, faithfulness calls for covenanted living within the community of faith for the life of God's world.

145

CHAPTER 13

Contemplation: Life as Ministry

Protestants have been supposing that religious work consists in *doing things for God*. We have been the active ones, planning what we think are the logical consequences, in action, of the gospel of Christ. And we have wanted God to be the passive receiver of our offerings, our services. But the time is come when we must go deeper, and learn that *God is the active one*, and learn that we are meant to be acted through. We must go down deeper, and discover, as a *way of living*, not as a belief, how to be *pliant*, how to *be worked through by God*, who has become a living internal dynamic deep within us. . . . the dynamic center of religion is in *God*, not in us; the world is in [God's] hands, not in ours; the center of creative living is in God, deep down with us as a *lived fact*, not in our heroic Nietzschean efforts to live *for* [God]. Over and around and within us all broods an active Love, or Life, a Presence, standing and knocking, in saint and sinner, regardless of environment. To that dynamic persuasive Love and Life we would yield our own little lives, and in bonded union with [God] *be worked through*, in joyful submission.

Thomas Kelly,
The Eternal Promise[1]

Beginning with listening, moving to imagination, prayer, dreams, and the mystical experience, what has been spoken of is contemplative practice. The reader has been encouraged to practice contemplation to gain a deeper understanding and faith in reality as

God-centered and a fuller participation in the purposes of God in Christ. In the midst of that understanding and participation a "yes" is called for, a conversion of faith from belief in a self-centered world view of the Enlightenment to the God-centered world view of the Bible.

Life lived with God as the central reality, the magnetic north to one's compass, the source of one's beginnings, the destination of life's journey, is a life of ministry. I am not speaking here of ordained ministry although some are called in their uniqueness to serve God in that way. Ministry is a calling to be who we are for God's purposes. Ministry involves recognition of God at our center and the development of the discipline of listening to God's call—listening for the subtle as well as the shouted words of the caring Creator calling us to follow in faith, reverence, and compassion to where God leads and is found. There we will find the reality of our lives, the realities of the lives of those we encounter, other people, other creatures, the whole living earth and the One in whom all dwell. In this reality there will always be beauty and bleakness, joy and suffering. There we are called to work with and for God's purposes with our unique gifts and needs, which is our ministry. There we will know joy found in real relationships and redefined hope in God with whom, through faith, we have cast our lot.

Christian spiritual life grows and deepens as we open to the mystery of grace, convert our faith object from self to God, and follow God's call. God's call is amplified and clarified in contemplation. As we go and grow toward where God calls the nature of our service will vary with our uniqueness but each of us will be in ministry.

A question is asked of those who encourage contemplation. Does contemplation of God and God's will and way lead to a clearer understanding of God's call, or does it encourage self-absorption to the exclusion of others? Contemplation, with its valuing of mystical experience, has been called navel-gazing by some, self-indulgent by others.

The testimony of contemplative geniuses of the Christian tradition tell us of the interdependence of contemplation and compassionate action in the service of human need and the stewardship of God's creation. The key seems to be whether one becomes deeply involved in the contemplation of self or God. The contemplation of God includes neighbor, self, and the whole of creation. The contemplation of self, as important as it is in maturing, is not enough for the maturation of our vision and our potential for righteousness.

Christian ministry is life lived to serve God and God's creation in the name and spirit of Jesus. It recognizes God at the center of all life and acknowledges our place as servants in partnership with God who was revealed in the servant life of Jesus, a new revelation of the nature of God's messianic method, a revelation confirmed in the resurrection.

It sounds demeaning, in a world where winning is everything, to be asked to assume a serving function. It is losing, a loss of pride and control that is hard to give up. The promise of Jesus is that in this losing, all that matters is gained.

The ultimate question asked of each of us upon the conclusion of our living is *Who did you serve?* Who we serve determines the direction of our lives' actions and their ultimate worth. Who we choose to serve is the basic faith decision upon which all else in our lives is measured. Christian ministry is life lived first and foremost to serve God as revealed in the person and way of Jesus Christ.

Contemplation and ministry are interdependent. If contemplation, that is religious openness, listening, revering of God, is faithfully practiced, it leads the listener to hear with greater clarity the call to ministry. As the call is followed the demands of ministry encourage greater and deeper contemplation of who and how we serve. Contemplation expands understanding, coordinates action, and provides reference for prioritizing values.

Geniuses of the Christian mysticism affirm the interrelationship and mutual dependence of contemplation and ministry, the being and doing of our lives. A few sterling examples of how these giants of the contemplative life came to understand this interrelationship follow.

Meister Eckhart

Eckhart, a Dominican friar, was born in 1260 in what is now Germany. He died in 1328. His abundant writing and recorded sermons are classics in Christian mystical thought. But his Pope condemned him as a heretic for his mystical bent, which distracted from papal authority. Eckhart's genius survives the years and transcends dogma. We hear Eckhart's mystical orientation toward all being one in God and see his similarity to eastern faiths in this piece taken from his *Sermon 6:*

> Nothing hinders the soul's knowledge of God as much as time and space, for time and space are fragments, whereas God is one! And, therefore, if the soul is to know God, it must know him above time and outside space; for God is neither this nor that as are these manifold things. God is One![2]

In *Sermon 23* Eckhart's often-quoted mystical insight concludes, "My eye and God's eye are one and the same—one in seeing, one in knowing and one in loving." It is from this oneness in loving that the movement from contemplation to servant living is made. Eckhart was asked a question of the relationship of the two. His answer,

> You may, however, say: "Alas, good man, if to be prepared for God one needs a heart freed from ideas and activities which are natural to the agents of the soul, how about those deeds that occupied St. Paul on behalf of the people, so much that he was like a father to them? Shall we be denied the [divine] goodness because we do virtuous deeds?" Let us see how this question is to be answered. The one [contemplation] is good. The other [deeds of virtue] is necessary. Mary was praised for having chosen the better part. But Martha's life was useful, for she waited on Christ and his disciples.[3]

In this same context Eckhart quotes St. Thomas Aquinas, who said that the "active life is better than the contemplative for in it one pours out the love he has received in contemplation." Eckhart expands upon Aquinas's thought: "Yet it is all one; for what we plant in the soil of contemplation we shall reap in the harvest of action and thus the purpose of contemplation is achieved."

John Ruysbroeck

Ruysbroeck was born in what is now known as Belgium in the village of Ruysbroeck in 1293. He entered the priesthood and was the chaplain to a cathedral in Brussels for many years. At the age

of fifty he left the traditional priesthood and adopted a more clois-
tered life, dedicating himself to contemplation and deeds of char-
itable and helpful action. Disciples gathered around him as they
identified with his disciplines and priorities. He lived to be
eighty-eight.

Ruysbroeck wrote,

> A man who lives this life, i.e., the active life, in its perfection, as
> it has here been shown, and who is offering up his whole life, and all
> his works, to the worship and praise of God, and who wills and
> loves God above all things, is often stirred by a desire to see, to know
> and to prove what, in Himself, this Bridegroom Christ is.[4]

Ruysbroeck illustrates this with the wonderful story of Zaccheus,
the tax collector in the New Testament who, abandoning all dignity, climbed a tree to catch a glimpse of Jesus of whom he had
heard so much and toward whom he poured his expectations.

> When the soul climbs with desire above the multiplicity of creatures
> and above the works of the senses, and above the light of nature,
> then it meets Christ. . . and becomes enlightened. . . . . When it
> stretches itself with longing towards this incomprehensible God,
> then it meets Christ, and is filled with his gifts. And when it loves
> and rests above all gifts, and above itself, and above all creatures,
> then it dwells in God and God dwells in it. This is the way in which
> we shall meet Christ on the summit of the active life. When you
> have laid the foundation of righteousness, charity and humility;
> and have established on it a dwelling place, this is, those virtues
> which have been named heretofore; and have met Christ through
> faith, by intention and by love, then you dwell in God and God
> dwells in you, and you possess the true active life.[5]

St. Teresa of Avila

St. Teresa lived in sixteenth-century Spain and is one of the names
on the list of geniuses of Spanish spirituality of the time, a list that
includes John of the Cross and Ignatius Loyola. Her message is
deeply mystical yet her life as a Carmelite nun was said to be the
consummate blending of Martha and Mary. Evelyn Underhill
commented on her blending of the contemplative and active life:
"She could turn from directions about the finances of the commu-

nity or the right sweeping down of the house, to deal in a manner equally wise and precise with the most delicate problems of the soul."[6]

Born the daughter of affluent and noble parents, her developing years were refined by the tension between the claim of the pleasures of the position her birth offered and the early and constant inclination to religious life she felt in her heart.

> On the one hand God was calling me. On the other, I was following the world. All the things of God gave me pleasure, yet I was tied and bound to those of the world. It seemed as if I wanted to reconcile these two contradictory things, . . . the life of the spirit and the pleasures and joys and pastimes of the senses. . . . I spent nearly twenty years on that stormy sea, often falling in this way and each time rising again, but to little purpose, as I would only fall once more.[7]

The Interior Castle, written as a guide to spiritual maturation for members of her order, is a classic in its genre. The metaphor of the interior life being a castle within came to her in answer to prayer and reflects Jesus words in the gospel of John, "In my Father's house are many rooms" (John 14:2 RSV). She writes of seven interior rooms or mansions, each one bringing the soul to more intimate experience and understanding of God. In the sixth room "the soul's faith and love are more stabilized. Prayer has become very precious, and it finds its joy in doing the will of God, no matter how difficult."[8]

The seventh room finds the soul at peace but not beyond temptations. Suffering and trials are never past, but in the seventh room peace reigns deep within one's heart. Jesus is the central revelation and teacher here. The way of the spirit in the world is recognized and chosen.

> Fix your eyes on the Crucified and nothing else will be of much importance to you. . . . Do you know when people really become spiritual? It is when they become slaves of God and are branded with his sign, which is the sign of the Cross, in token that they have given Him their freedom.[9]

With the insights of woman's liberation, so consistent with the liberation of the spirit Christ gives, as was given St. Teresa, her call to slavery may sound a dissonant cord to modern ears. I suspect that the liberation of women from male domination in our time is not unlike the struggle that St. Teresa went through as she chose between the ways of her world and the ways of her faith. They were the struggles encountered in the first room in the interior castle. The spiritual insights of later rooms does not deny the truth of modern liberation movements. It acknowledges the deeper truth of Christ that when we have given ourselves over to God's purposes, lost our life as it were, we find our life. Liberation is never spiritually appropriate as an end in itself although always a necessary step in the journey of the soul. The essential question of liberation is, *Free for what purpose?* St. Teresa never left the world into which she was born, yet transcended it. In the end she reconciled that world and the world of the Spirit in her work and contemplation.

Evelyn Underhill

Born in 1875 in London, Evelyn Underhill was a daughter of the establishment. Her father was a noted lawyer. Their home was proper but not religious. She wrote to a friend, "I wasn't brought up to religion."[10] She was bright and gained success as a student at Kings College, London, an education that exposed her to various disciplines in the humanities, including theology and the history of religion. Gradually she came to honor the Christian faith through the great minds and writers of the tradition and took it as her own. Her path led to mysticism and resulted in an early and profound book on the subject, *Mysticism* (1911). She wrote in many fields, including fiction, theology, philosophy, education, poetry, and spiritual direction. Her own spiritual journey moved from a theocentric faith to a Christocentric faith. In 1927 she wrote,

> Until about five years ago I never had any personal experience of our Lord. . . . I was a convinced Theocentric, . . . I had, from time to time, what seemed to be vivid experiences of God, from the time of my conversion from agnosticism (about twenty years ago now) . . . I went to the Baron [Baron Friedrich von Hugel, an eminent Roman Catholic theologian]. . . . Somehow by his prayers or something he compelled me to experience Christ. . . . The New Testament, which once I couldn't make much of, or meditate on, now seems full of things I never noticed.[11]

Throughout her life of faith the mystical vision was the touch-stone of her religious understanding. From her initial conversion to belief in God to the refinement and illumination of that vision in a glorious understanding of Jesus as the Christ, the harmony and grace of the mystical vision informed the core of her faith. It was a vision, refined by her devotion to Jesus as the Christ, that led her into the world rather than from it.

> The real mark of spiritual triumph—the possession of that more lovely, more abundant life which we discern in moments of deep prayer—is not an abstraction from this world, but a return to it; a willing use of its conditions as material for the expression of love. There is nothing high-minded about Christian holiness. It is most at home in the slum, the street, the hospital ward. . . . A little water, some fragments of bread, and a chalice of wine are enough to close the gap between two worlds, and give the soul and senses a trembling contact with the Eternal Charity. By means of these its creatures, that touch still cleanses, and that hand still feeds.[12]

Thomas Merton

Merton, the Trappist monk who came to be the voice of the religious activists of the 1960s and 1970s, was our contemporary. He integrates rational and intuitive thought, secular and spiritual experience. From his book, *Contemplation in a World of Action*, he echoes the mystics of the past and calls us into our futures.

> Real Christian living is stunted and frustrated if it remains content with the bare externals of worship, with "saying prayers" and "going to church," with fulfilling one's external duties and merely being respectable. The real purpose of prayer. . . . is the deepening of personal realization in love, the awareness of God. . . . The real purpose of meditation . . . is the exploration and discovery of new dimensions in freedom, illumination and love, in deepening our awareness of our life in Christ.
>   . . . he who attempts to act and do things for others or for the world without deepening his own self-understanding, freedom, integrity and capacity to love, will not have anything to give others. He will communicate to them nothing but the contagion of his own obsessions, his aggressiveness, his ego-centered ambitions, his delusions about ends and means, his doctrinaire prejudices and ideas.

153

As Merton speaks to the activists of the need for grounding in contemplation, he speaks to the contemplative, calling for actions of "selfless love."

> One of the paradoxes of the mystical life is this: that a man cannot enter into the deepest center of himself and pass through that center into God, unless he is able to pass entirely out of himself and empty himself and give himself to other people in the purity of selfless love.
>
> And so one of the worst illusions in the life of contemplation would be to try to find God by barricading yourself inside your own soul, shutting out all external reality by sheer concentration and willpower, cutting yourself off from the world and other [people] by shutting yourself inside your own mind and closing the door like a turtle.[13]

Called from Our Centers

Finally, and paradoxically (isn't all truth best spoken in paradox?), the call that comes to each of us is to lose our lives in and for God's love with the promise that by so doing we will find our lives. The call is from the center of existence to our center, the mysterious meeting of Self and self. It depends upon the development of our listening skills to hear the call more clearly, listening to God, to neighbor, to self. It depends upon our imaginations to entertain new and expanding possibilities. The call speaks throughout dreams, acquainting us with our whole selves, our shadow and our light, our anxieties and our abilities. Our prayers bring us into closer relationship not only with God who calls but also with ourselves, continuing our growth in spirit and Truth to greater and greater freedom to give ourselves in love to serve God's purposes.

Again, the promise in the call is that if we lose our lives to God's purposes we will find them. What is found is not a perfected version of the crude material that was our self, refined by the divine fires. What is found is grace—accepting, serving, footwashing, cross-bearing, resurrecting grace. When we have looked into and beyond ourselves to where our love and our lives may be given, and when we have given them, all aspect of our lives, dross and precious, will be seen as essential in the service of life. When we have allowed ourselves to open to the mystery, when we have heard the call of God and have followed, we will understand the importance of our individual lives, the value of our unique selves. Life will not then be easier, necessarily, but more joyful. Life will not be safer but more adventurous. Life will not be without sorrow but will be more meaningful. We will be freer than ever we could have been. We will be freer to develop all the parts of our selves and offer our whole selves—heart, mind, and soul—in the love and service of God and God's creation, our ministry.

We who are the inclusive evangelical churches will find our lives as churches as we affirm the truth that God is the center of existence, call our members and those who would join with us to belief in the good news of the grace of God who dwells in mystery at the center and throughout all creation.

The essential ministry of the churches is evangelism. The ministries of the individual members are as varied as the gifts and the circumstances with which they find themselves. The whole enterprise turns on the central realities of God's existence and God's grace.

The hope for churches, particularly the inclusive evangelical churches who have been in the mainstream in recent history but are no longer, is in knowing that God is at center, developing the capacity to live in the uncertainty of the mystery of grace, which is faith, and in following where God calls, which is our ministry.

Appendix

Living Faith

A course outline for a spiritual growth and faithful living group in a local church.

Group Size

In local church settings groups using the Living Faith format have been kept to a number that enables them to hear one another around a circle. There should be time for all to contribute to a general discussion. Between sixteen to twenty-four members works; a lower number is possible, but a higher number makes it difficult for group dynamics. Three to four members of each group's total are leaders.

Leaders

The leadership has been composed of lay and ordained persons who have been through the course at least once. A minimum of two lay leaders and a maximum of two ordained leaders has been maintained. The leaders participate in their group as participant members as well as leaders.

Leadership Involves

1. Set dates, times, and locations for weekly group meetings and course-ending retreat

2. Meet before the course begins to plan publicity and recruitment
3. Meet for approximately two hours between group sessions for
   a. evaluation of the previous session
   b. planning for the next
      1. planning for each session involves creating an agenda designating activities and leadership functions for the session and
      2. agreeing on responsibilities, individual and shared
4. Pay attention to every group member to determine interest, well being, progress and special needs

Sample agenda for first session:

Living Faith Group
Series 1
Session 1

7:30 p.m.	Introduce ourselves and tell why we are in the course	(Margie)
8:00	Devotions Isa. 55:1–3a, 6–13	(Bill)
8:25	Review commitments to be made by leaders and by members (copy of commitments and other information mailed to members before first session)	(Becky)
8:30	Break (refreshments provided by two leaders for first session. Sign-up for refreshments for following sessions put on table)	
8:40	Listening Training	
	1. Introducing listening as spiritual disciple	(Carmelle)
	2. Leaders demonstrate listening groups of three, listener, listened to, and observer introduced	(Becky)
	3. Divide group into listening training groups	(Becky)
9:10	Report back from listening groups	(Margie)
9:20	Pass out assignment for daily work: reading chapter on listening and	

| | daily entry in journal | (Bill) |
| 9:25 | Closing devotion | (Carmelle) |

Group Commitments

Leaders
1. to begin and end the session on time
2. to participate fully in the group life and exercises in the pursuit of their own spiritual growth
3. to attend the weekly sessions and the retreat, and not to miss more than one session during the span of the course
4. to honor all discussion in group as confidential
5. to be available to group members both during and between group sessions
6. to meet regularly before each session and the retreat to plan and evaluate
7. to use the leadership meetings not only for planning but also for opportunities to share and support each other in their life and faith

Members
1. to attend each session and the retreat. If, for reasons beyond one's control, sessions have to be missed, it is understood that missing more than two sessions means that one must drop out of the course. One may take it another time
2. to arrive on time
3. to do the daily assignments between the weekly meetings
4. to keep the discussion in the group confidential
5. to pay the fees agreed upon to cover the costs of materials and the retreat, including leaders' costs

Outline of Ten-Week Session and Retreat

Session 1: Meeting one another and introduction of listening
1. Introducing ourselves
2. Opening devotion: scripture focus, Isa. 55:1–3a, 6–13
3. Review commitments
4. Break
5. Listening introduced

6. Listening triads
7. Chapter on listening assigned with daily reading suggestions and journal entry responses encouraged
8. Closing devotion

Session 2: Listening training continued, meditation as devotional listening introduced

1. Opening devotion: scripture focus, Luke 8:4–8
2. Report back of week's reading and responses in whole group
3. Listening training continued
   a. types of listening
   b. blocks to listening
   c. new listening triads
4. Break
5. Meditation
   a. introduced and taught
   b. practiced
6. Myers-Briggs Personality Type Preference[1] instrument introduced; questions and answer sheets given to each member to be completed this week
7. Chapter on imagination assigned with daily reading suggestions and journal entry responses encouraged
8. Closing devotion

Session 3: Imagination in relationship to faith experience

1. Opening devotion: guided meditation on John 8:1–11
2. Introduce Quaker Dialogue group discussion method
   a. a question is asked of whole group, in this instance questions having to do with individual's experience of imagination such as, "Has your imagination been helpful or harmful in your life? How? "
   b. each member given opportunity to respond or pass
   c. key contribution of group members is focused— listening in silence
   d. no comment or response to contributions are to be made
   e. volunteer is first to speak in response to the question and says "done" when finished
   f. following clockwise around the circle members pass or respond
3. Quaker Dialogue

4. Break—collect Myers-Briggs answers
5. Journaling methods introduced (based on *At An Intensive Journal Workshop* by Ira Progoff)[2]
    a. general journal use introduction
    b. dialogue method of journaling taught
    c. using John 8:1–11, dialogue with one or more roles of story
        1. persecutors
        2. victim
        3. redeemer/forgiver
6. Opportunity to comment in whole group on journal work
7. Chapter on prayer assigned with suggested daily reading and journal response
8. Closing devotion

Session 4:   Prayer as practice and attitude
1. Opening devotion: scripture focus a selection on prayer, such as Mark 9: 14–29
2. Open discussion on chapter on prayer
3. Break
4. Myers-Briggs
    a. pass out our preference scores from Myers-Briggs
    b. explain scoring method and interpret
    c. affirm legitimacy of each score and various ways individuals perceive and process information
    d. use Myers-Briggs to show that each member comes to his or her faith differently and each approach is legitimate, no goal of archetypal sainthood
5. Prayerful touch
    a. various nonverbal trust games can be used
    b. some form of laying on of hands used with emphasis upon loving and prayerful concern expressed in touch
6. Group discussion of prayerful touch
7. Chapter on dreams assigned with suggested daily reading and journal response plus using journal to keep track of dreams. Partners assigned for contact and conversation twice during week.
8. Closing devotion

Session 5:   Dreams and introduction of shadow
1. Opening devotions: Scripture focus Acts 2:14–18

2. Discussion of week's reading in small groups or in group as a whole
3. Leaders demonstrate a dream group process using one of their dreams
4. Break
5. Introduce Jungian concept of shadow
   a. childhood fears
      1. begin with each writing in journal a list of fears remembered
      2. open discussion telling of fears as members choose to participate
   b. adult fears
      1. use journal to make two lists of present fears
         a. what I fear I may be capable of
         b. what I fear I am incapable of
      2. discussion of this work can be in small groups or group as a whole
   c. explore the Myers-Briggs preference scores in relation to what one is comfortable with and fearful of
6. Introduce concept of projection
   a. a leader tells of a fear and how it was projected upon another
   b. group response
7. Assignment for the following two weeks is based on the discussion of the shadow in the dream chapter. The theme for the two-week assignment is Acknowledging and Accepting Our Shadow. It is suggested that the days' assignments alternate between reading with journal reflections and conversations with the assigned partner. A different partner each week deepens relationships in the group. (Following this outline of weekly sessions are some readings and assignments for the shadow work that have been used in the course.)
8. Closing devotion

Session 6: Shadow work continued
1. Opening devotion: Scripture focus John 1:1–5
2. Begin the discussion of the shadow work by dividing into three groups to discuss our wounds. Individuals can report back to the whole group as they choose
3. Break
4. Shadow projection—journal work

  a. Think of a person you do not like
  b. What about him or her is offensive?
  c. What do you feel when you are with him or her?
  d. What fear do you have that this relationship accentuates?
  e. Open opportunity for sharing in the larger group without pressure to share

5. A leader is encouraged at this point to lead a discussion on how the grace of God works when one confesses destructive behavior, begins to understand the fear that is behind it and the benefit of accepting responsibility for the care of one's own vulnerabilities. Ways of taking care of one's vulnerabilities spiritually and psychologically are best understood if specific stories are told by leaders or by other members of the group

6. New partners for second week of shadow work are assigned

7. Closing devotion

Session 7:   Concluding shadow work, introducing the light side

1. Opening devotion: Scripture focus Matthew 5:14ff.

2. Quaker Dialogue—question: "Where has your shadow work led you?"

3. Break

4. Leader introduces concept of light that is in us
  a. Quaker concept of divine light within
  b. Genesis 1 exclamation of God at each step of creation including that of human beings
  c. To say we have light within us does not mean that we are without darkness. We are not talking purity here

5. Journal collage of light
  The following requests are made one at a time with time given to write after each. Each participant is asked to pray before beginning to write a response using these words: *Help me to understand the light I know and possess.*
  a. List five ways you particularly like that you express light in your life
  b. Remember and record a joyful time in your life
  c. List things that are fun for you to do. Select your favorite
  d. Tell of a time you felt the presence of God

    e. Finally, read over your four responses. After reading them, summarize with your group any insight that presented itself

6. Open discussion of journal collage exercise
7. Partners are assigned to make contact twice during the next week. The week's exercise is on gifts that come from our light and shadow. (Following this outline, session suggestions for this assignment are given.)
8. Closing devotion: Scripture focus 2 Cor. 4:6

Session 8:   Imaginative Bible Work: The Parable of the Forgiving Father

1. Opening devotion: Scripture focus Luke 15:11–24
2. An extended exploration of the forgiveness of God as revealed in the parable of the prodigal son and the forgiving father is suggested using various methods of experiencing and understanding God's love. These include
   a. nonverbal body positions to represent various stages of the child and parent experience throughout the story
   b. art materials of various sorts to give expression to feelings and insights
   c. small group dramatizing parable in a contemporary setting
3. Break
4. Experiences of God's love in the lives of group members
   a. begin with journaling
   b. choose some form of general discussion
5. Assignment for this week's daily work is to read designated sections of chapter on conversion. Respond daily in journal. Partners may or may not be assigned as leaders choose
6. Closing devotion

Session 9:   Calling: The Concept and Experience

1. Opening devotion: Scripture focus Isa. 6:1–8
2. Discussion in small groups or group as a whole on reading of past week
3. Break
4. Introduce concept of a calling
   a. two basic types of call are
      1. from within

2. from other's expectations
   b. Develop a group process to explore calls we hear and respond to
   c. One possible way to proceed is to discuss roles we play and whether they are in response to calls from within, from others, or from combination of each
   d. Which roles bring us most pleasure?
5. Explore in group how one discerns God's call
6. Assignment for daily work is to read the final two chapters of this book on the mystical experience and life as ministry
7. Closing devotion

Session 10:   Retreat

A twenty-four-hour retreat over a Friday night has worked well beginning with Friday dinner and concluding mid- to late Saturday afternoon.

The goals of the retreat are:

1. to affirm one another as beloved children of God with unique and special gifts
2. to support one another as each works to find and give expression to what God is calling him or her to be and do at this stage of life
3. to worship, relax, continue working on developing and demonstrating a living faith, and enjoy one another

Three main activities have been a part of each Living Faith retreat

1. Friday evening self portrait using whatever media or method the leaders of the group prefer
2. A Saturday morning valentine session
   a. Each member is given as many blank cards as there are members in the group and a list of the group members' names
   b. They are given an hour or more to write a note of appreciation to each member recognizing the specific gifts each one has
   c. Envelopes with the names of group members are provided. Completed cards are placed in them
   d. When all cards are completed, the envelopes are passed to whom they are addressed

    e. A quiet time is provided for each to go off and read the valentines

3. Late Saturday morning members are invited to go off by themselves and do journal work on the following three questions:

    a. To what is God calling me?

    b. What is the first step?

    c. What support do I need in order to continue as God would have me go?

4. Early Saturday afternoon Quaker Dialogue or some other method of group discussion of the journal work concludes the agenda except for the concluding worship

5. Two major worship experiences happen on the retreat:

    a. Saturday morning communion before breakfast

    b. closing worship, which is created by volunteers of the group who on Friday night agree to prepare and lead it

Resources for Daily Exercises for Sessions Five, Six and Seven:

John A. Sanford
Jesus, Paul, and Depth Psychology

The Persona and the Shadow

There is a mask we all wear which Jungian psychology calls the "persona." The persona is the face we present to the world, and also, much of the time, to ourselves. We want people to think of us in a certain way, and so we assume a pose which will give people that impression of us. We wear a mask, hoping others cannot see behind this mask to those dark corners in us which we want to keep hidden.

In contrast to the persona is that part of our personality which Jung called the "shadow." The shadow is that part of ourselves which contradicts our ego ideal. It includes all those dark aspects of ourselves which stand in contrast to the person we ideally want to be. The shadow is always in contrast to the persona. For instance, if we strike a pose of being a kind and loving person, the shadow personality will appear as the personification of everything within us which contradicts that. The shadow is thus like another personality within us of which we are more or less afraid.

When our attempt to escape from our shadow is accomplished on a purely unconscious level, we speak of "repression." Repression is an unconscious mechanism in us which banishes from consciousness whatever it is about ourselves which is too difficult or unpleasant to face. . . .

But here is where depth psychology comes into the picture with some disturbing news: repression is not a solution to our psychological and spiritual conflicts. The shadow does not cease to exist merely because it is banished from consciousness. To the contrary, the shadow continues to live on in us in the unconscious, and becomes increasingly like another, quite distinct personality from our usual conscious personality. . . .

We are not the only one who pays a price for the repression of the shadow; repression of the shadow has grievous social consequences as well. The shadow personality may become projected onto other people, that is, we may see in them the envy, greed, selfishness, pride, etc., which we do not admit are part of our own make-up. This causes an enormous distortion of personal and social relationships, for if we see in someone else the shadowy characteristics which belong to us, but which we have not faced, we will react to that person in paranoid hate or fear.[3]

Fritz Kunkel
In Search of Maturity

Expression of what we find within ourselves, honest and reckless expression before the face of the Eternal, assuming responsibility for what we are, even if we are unaware of it, and asking God to help us to master the wild horse, or to revive the skeletons of horses which we dig out during the long hours of our confessions—this is the psychological method of religious self-education. It is a way of bringing to consciousness our unconscious contents, and of establishing control over our hidden powers. It is the way to mature responsibility. It is the old way of the psalmist: "Yet who can detect his lapses? Absolve me from my faults unknown! And hold thy servant back from willful sins, from giving way to them" (Psalm 9:12, 13, Moffat).[4]

David E. Roberts
Psychotherapy and a Christian View of Man

We reach security only by a trustful acceptance of the full truth about ourselves and others, not by evasion of it. Healing power is latent in humans because it is latent "in the nature of things." Hence it is not surprising that men and women have found in Christ the supreme disclosure of what coincidence between human beatitude and divine love means. Christ is Savior as He opens, for each person, the way whereby that individual can move toward such coincidence. This involves moving forward into a deepened recognition of failure, impotence and need at many points.

But the divine forgiveness which He discloses always has been and always will be accessible to us. We experience divine forgiveness as the "making right" of our lives which occurs when we turn away from fighting ourselves, and others, and the truth itself, and turn trustfully toward the divine power which surrounds us and can work through us.

This experience of reconciliation, despite past failures and unsolved problems in the present, makes persons actually more lovable, more discerning, more capable of devoting themselves to goods which enrich all humanity.[5]

Charles B. Hanna
The Face of the Deep

We cannot stand the sight of our dark side, so we repress it, push it under, thinking we have thereby disposed of it. But we have not. We have simply pushed it into a place where it both has us in its grip and automatically projects itself on the person or the nation we do not like; *so the tension we will not stand in ourselves* is carelessly and irresponsibly cast out to increase the tension and strife and anguish of our world. . . . Jung saw it as a psychological law that what we will not suffer inwardly through conscious recognition of our shadow, we will suffer outwardly as the result of our unconscious projections into the world around us. He thereby gives Christians the most awesome charge that they can possibly receive throughout their lives: the withdrawal of their projections upon others, and dealing with their shadow themselves.[6]

Appendix

Carl G. Jung
Psychology and Religion

We must still be exceedingly careful in order not to reject our own shadows too shamelessly. We are still swamped with projected illusions. If you imagine someone who is brave enough to withdraw those projections, all and sundry, then you get an individual conscious of a pretty thick shadow.

Such a man has saddled himself with new problems and conflicts. He has become a serious problem to himself as he is now unable to say that "they" do this or that, "they" are wrong, and "they" must be fought against. He lives in a house of "self-collection." Such a man knows that whatever is wrong in the world is in himself and if he only learns to deal with his own shadow, then he has done something real for the world.

He is succeeding in removing an infinitesimal part at least of the unsolved gigantic social problems of our day. These problems are unwieldy and poised by mutual projections.[7]

Lauren van der Post
Jung, The Story of Our Time

The answer as Jung saw it was to abolish tyranny, to enthrone, as it were, two opposites side by side in the service of the master pattern, not *opposing or resisting* evil, but *transforming and redeeming* it. These two opposites in the negations of our time could be turned into tragic enemies but truly seen psychologically and again defined best, perhaps, in the non-emotive terms of physics, they were like the negative and positive inductions of energy observed in the dynamics of electricity; the two parallel and opposite streams, without the flash of lightning, for me always the symbol of awareness made imperative, was impossible.[8]

H. William Gregory

With every shadow aspect there is a gift from that shadow. For example, if a shadow aspect is insecurity, one of the gifts of that insecurity could be empathy for others who suffer from some degree of insecurity. This empathy is dependent upon your acceptance and understanding of your own insecurity. But once faced and accepted as a part of you the gift of empathy can be experienced. Others who are insecure are less troublesome for you because they no longer are reminders of unaccepted insecurity in yourself.

Empathy thus becomes an aspect of your light side. List the dominant shadow aspects of yourself and opposite them see what gifts of light are present in you or could be present in you if you accept the shadow as part of yourself and not project it upon others.

Theologically your ability to accept your shadow is based upon your trust of God's love for you. The more you understand that God loves all of who you are the less frightening the shadows become and their gifts become more available. This is an important aspect of what we know as the forgiveness of God.

Record your thoughts on your shadow, its gifts and God's forgiveness in your journal.

With every tension between shadow and light there is a temptation as well as a gift. Recognizing the temptations that arise from the tension is a gift in itself. It allows us to make better choices in responding to the temptations.

For example, if the shadow aspect is insecurity and the light side gift is empathy, the temptation from the shadow side could be to be judgmental of those who are insecure or to have a tendency to evade standing up for yourself.

There are two steps to today's exercise:
1. List the shadow and its gift and then determine as best you can what the temptation from the shadow side could be.
2. Compare the light side gift and see if it offers a way to cope with the temptation.[9]

Carl G. Jung
The Development of Personality

There are, besides the gifts of the head, also those of the heart, which are no whit less important, although they may easily be overlooked because in such cases the head is often the weaker organ. And yet people of this kind sometimes contribute more to the well-being of society, and are more valuable, than those with other talents.[10]

Notes

Chapter 1

1. H. Richard Niebuhr, *Radical Monotheism and Western Culture* (New York: Harper and Row, 1960), 32.
2. Ibid., 32.
3. Sydney Ahlstrom, *A Religious History of the American People* (New Haven: Yale University Press, 1972), 843.

Chapter 2

1. Wade Clark Roof and William McKinney, *American Mainline Religion* (New Brunswick: Rutgers University Press, 1987), 240.
2. Robert S. Michaelsen and Wade Clark Roof, "Liberal Protestantism: A Sociodemographic Perspective," in *Liberal Protestantism: Realities and Possibilities,* ed. Robert S. Michaelsen and Wade Clark Roof (New York: Pilgrim Press, 1986), 37ff.
3. Gibson Winter, *The New Creation as Metropolis* (New York: Macmillan, 1963). Although raised in the faith to work and look for the Kingdom of God, recent discomfort with the dominant male reference to God leads me to use instead the realm of God.
4. Harvey Cox, *The Secular City* (New York: Macmillan, 1965).
5. George Webber, *God's Colony in Man's World* (New York: Abingdon Press, 1960).
6. Phillip E. Hammond, "The Extravasation of the Sacred and the Crisis in Liberal Protestantism," in *Liberal Protestantism,* ed. Michaelsen and Roof, 51–64.

Chapter 3

1. Robert Wuthnow, *Restructuring of American Religion* (Princeton: Princeton University Press, 1988), 148.

2. Dorothy Bass, "Reflections on the Reports of Decline in Mainstream Protestantism," *The Chicago Theological Seminary Register* 80, no. 3 (Summer 1989): 5ff.

Chapter 4

1. Thomas Kelly, *The Eternal Promise*, 2d ed. (Richmond, Ind.: Friends United Press, 1988).

Chapter 5

1. M. Scott Peck, *The Different Drum: Community Making and Peace* (New York: Simon and Schuster, Inc., 1988), 86.

Chapter 6

1. William Wordsworth. "The World Is Too Much With Us," in *Masterpieces of Religious Verse*, ed. James Dalton Morrison (New York: Harper and Row, 1948), 94.
2. Robert E. Ornstein, *The Psychology of Consciousness* (New York: The Viking Press, 1972), 10.
3. John Waters, *The Man Who Killed the Deer* (Chicago: Swallow Press, Inc., 1970).
4. More can be learned of Ellis and Godfrey Chips in a book by John Lame Deer and Richard Erdoes, *Lame Deer, Seeker of Visions* (New York: Simon and Schuster, 1972). For example, the book contains an account of Godfrey telling a father and mother where and when they would find their lost child. Godfrey had a vision that told him the boy drowned in the Missouri River and would be washed ashore at a particular place and time. The family found their boy's body as Godfrey predicted. The Chips family told me the story was true.
5. Ornstein, *Psychology of Consciousness*, 60.
6. Ibid., 107.
7. Pierre Teilhard de Chardin, *The Phenomenon of Man* (New York: Harper and Row, 1975), 56.
8. Pierre Teilhard de Chardin, *The Divine Milieu* (New York: Harper and Row, 1960), 89.

Chapter 7

1. "The Unchurched American Ten Years Later," a study conducted by The Gallup Organization for Congress 88 and the Princeton Religion Research Center, Princeton, N.J., 1988.

2. Robert Bellah et al., *Habits of the Heart: Individualism and Commitment in America* (Berkeley and Los Angeles: University of California Press, 1985), 220–21.

3. Søren Kierkegaard, *Purity of Heart* (New York: Harper and Brothers, 1948).

4. Martin Buber, *I and Thou* (New York: Charles Scribner's Sons, 1970).

Chapter 8

1. Rainer Maria Rilke, *Duino Elegies and The Sonnets to Orpheus*, trans. A. Poulin, Jr. (Boston: Houghton Mifflin, 1977), 139.

2. Ibid., 61.

3. C. S. Lewis, *Letters to Malcolm: Chiefly on Prayer* (New York: Harcourt, Brace and World, Inc., 1963), 10.

4. Theodore Reik, *Listening with the Third Ear* (New York: Grove Press, 1948), 153.

5. Buber, *I and Thou*, 67.

6. Herbert Benson, *The Relaxation Response* (New York: William Morrow and Co., Inc., 1975), 78–79.

7. M. C. Richards, *Centering, In Pottery, Poetry, and the Person* (Middletown, Conn.: Wesleyan University Press, 1964), 9.

Chapter 9

1. Harold Clarke Goddard, *Alphabet of the Imagination* (Atlantic Highlands, N.J.: Humanities Press, 1974), 4.

2. William Blake, "Auguries of Innocence," in *The Complete Poetry and Prose of William Blake* (Berkeley and Los Angeles: University of California Press, 1982), 493.

3. Goddard, *Alphabet*, 91.

4. William Blake, "The Tiger," in ibid., 24.

5. Ira Progoff, *At An Intensive Journal Workshop* (New York: Dialogue House Library, 1975).

6. M. C. Richards, *Centering*, 12.

Chapter 10

1. Gerald Heard, *Ten Questions on Prayer*, Pendle Hill Pamphlet no. 58, Pendle Hill Publications, Wallingford, Pa., February 1951.

2. Carl G. Jung, *The Undiscovered Self* (Boston: Atlantic-Little, Brown, 1958), 84.

3. Henri J. Nouwen, *Pray to Live* (Notre Dame: Fides/Claretian, 1972), 24.

4. Thomas Merton, *New Seeds of Contemplation* (New York: New Directions, 1972), 25.

5. Samuel Miller, *The Life of the Soul* (New York: Harper and Brothers, 1951), 21.

6. Martin Buber, found quoted on a poster without reference to its origin.

7. Thomas Merton, *The Seven Story Mountain* (New York: New American Library Paperback, 1963), 185.

8. Nouwen, *Pray to Live*, 20.

9. Ibid.

10. John McGee, *Reality and Prayer* (New York: Harper and Row, 1957), 48.

Chapter 11

1. John A. Sanford, *Dreams: God's Forgotten Language* (Philadelphia: J. B. Lippincott Co., 1968).

2. Langston Hughes, "Hold Fast To Dreams," *The Langston Hughes Reader* (New York: G. Braziller, 1958).

3. Carl G. Jung, *Two Essays on Analytical Psychology* (New York: Princeton University Press, 1982), 126.

4. Ibid., 97.

5. Elizabeth Barrett Browning, "Aurora Leigh," in *Earth's Crammed With Heaven: Masterpieces of Religious Verse*, ed. James Dalton Morrison (New York: Harper and Row, 1948), 16.

6. Ann and Barry Ulanov, *Religion and the Unconscious* (Philadelphia: Westminster Press, 1975), 15.

7. Carl G. Jung, *Psychology and Religion* (New Haven: Yale University Press, 1966), 38.

8. John Neihardt, *Black Elk Speaks* (Lincoln: University of Nebraska Press, 1979).

9. Carl G. Jung, *Psychology and Religion*, 93, 95.

10. Laurens van der Post, *Jung and the Story of Our Time* (New York: Vintage Books, 1977), 238.

Chapter 12

1. As quoted by Vera Brittain in "Testament of Friendship," in F. C. Happold, *Mysticism* (Baltimore: Penguin Books, 1975), 131.

2. Merton, *New Seeds*, 14.

3. Happold, *Mysticism*, 45.

4. Margaret Isherwood, "The Root of the Matter," ibid., 129.

5. Brittain, "Testament of Friendship," ibid., 131.

6. William James, *The Varieties of Religious Experience* (New York: Mentor Books, 1961), 306.

7. Simone Weil, *Waiting for God* (New York: G. P. Putnam's Sons, 1951).

8. Ibid., 69.

9. Ibid., 72.

10. Ibid., 76.

11. Augustine, *The Confessions of Saint Augustine,* trans. F. J. Sheed (New York: Sheed and Ward, 1951), 145.

Chapter 13

1. Kelly, *Eternal Promise,* 44–45.

2. Raymond B. Blakney, trans., *Meister Eckhart—A Modern Translation* (New York: Harper and Row, 1941), 131.

3. *Sermon 23,* ibid., 206.

4. John Ruysbroeck, from *The Culmination of the Active Life,* quoted in *Mysticism,* ed. F. C. Happold (Baltimore: Penguin Books, 1975), 282.

5. Ibid., 283.

6. Evelyn Underhill, *The Mystics of the Church* (New York: George H. Doran, 1926), 176.

7. E. Allison Peers, trans., *The Life of St. Teresa of Jesus* (Garden City, N.J.: Doubleday, 1960), 105, 108.

8. Bernhard Christensen, *The Inward Pilgrimage* (Minneapolis: Augsburg, 1976), 61.

9. Teresa of Avila, *The Interior Castle,* trans. E. Allison Peers (Garden City, N.J.: Doubleday Image Books, 1961), 229.

10. Charles Williams, ed., *The Letters of Evelyn Underhill* (New York: Longmans, Green, 1953), 4.

11. Margaret Cropper, *Life of Evelyn Underhill* (New York: Harper and Brothers, 1958), 9.

12. Evelyn Underhill, *The School of Charity* (New York: David McKay, 1934), 67.

13. Thomas Merton, *Contemplation in a World of Action* (Garden City, N.J.: Image Books, 1923), 178–79.

Appendix

1. The Myers-Briggs Type Indicator is an instrument widely used to aid individuals gain understanding of how they perceive and process information. It is valuable in that it affirms all methods of perception and process and guides individuals to recognize the worth of other ways practiced by other individuals. It is a helpful instrument for faith devel-

opment groups as it illustrates various ways to recognize and respond to information, be it rational or intuitive. MBTI, Consulting Psychologists Press, Inc., 577 College Avenue, Palo Alto, CA 94306.

2. Ira Progoff, *At an Intensive Journal Workshop* (New York: Dialogue House Library, 1975).

3. John A. Sanford, *Jesus, Paul, and Depth Psychology* (King of Prussia, Pa.: Religious Publishing House, 1974), 55–56.

4. Fritz Kunkel, *In Search of Maturity* (New York: Charles Scribner's Sons, 1943), 253–54.

5. David E. Roberts, *Psychotherapy and a Christian View of Man* (New York: Charles Scribner's Sons, 1950), 135.

6. Charles B. Hanna, *The Face of the Deep* (Philadelphia: Westminster Press, 1967), 100–101.

7. Jung, *Psychology and Religion*, 101–2.

8. van der Post, *Jung*, 218.

9. II. William Gregory, from unpublished course material used in Living Faith courses.

10. Carl G. Jung, *The Development of Personality*, vol. 17 of *Collected Works of C. G. Jung* (Princeton, N.J.: Princeton University Press, 1985), 140.

Bibliography

Ahlstrom, Sydney. *A Religious History of the American People*. New Haven: Yale University Press, 1972.

Bass, Dorothy. "Reflections on the Reports of Decline in Mainstream Protestantism." *The Chicago Theological Seminary Register* 80, no. 3 (Summer 1989).

Bellah, Robert, et al. *Habits of the Heart, Individualism and Commitment in America*. Berkeley, Los Angeles: University of California Press, 1985.

Benson, Herbert. *The Relaxation Response*. New York: William Morrow and Co., Inc., 1975.

Blake, William. *The Complete Poetry and Prose of William Blake*. Berkeley and Los Angeles: University of California Press, 1982.

Blakney, Robert B., trans. *Meister Eckhart—A Modern Translation*. New York: Harper and Row, 1941.

Bonhoeffer, Dietrich. *The Cost of Discipleship*. New York: Macmillan Co., 1964.

Briggs-Myers, Isabel. *Myers-Briggs Type Indicator*. Palo Alto, Calif.: Consulting Psychologists Press, 1976.

Browning, Elizabeth Barrett. *Earth's Crammed with Heaven: Masterpieces of Religious Verse*. Edited by James Dalton Morrison. New York: Harper and Row, 1948.

Buber, Martin. *I and Thou*. New York: Charles Scribner's Sons, 1970.

Christensen, Bernhard. *The Inward Pilgrimage*, Minneapolis, Minn.: Augsburg, 1976,

Cox, Harvey. *The Secular City.* New York: Macmillan, 1965.

Cropper, Margaret. *Life of Evelyn Underhill*. New York: Harper and Brothers, 1958.

Goddard, Harold Clarke. *Alphabet of the Imagination*. Atlantic Highlands, N.J.: Humanities Press, 1974.

Hammond, Phillip E. "The Extravasation of the Sacred and the Crisis in

Liberal Protestantism." In *Liberal Protestantism*, edited by Robert Michaelsen and Wade Clark Roof. New York: Pilgrim Press, 1986.

Hanna, Charles B. *The Face of the Deep*. Philadelphia: Westminster Press, 1967.

Happold, F. C. *Mysticism*. Baltimore: Penguin Books, 1975.

Heard, Gerald. *Ten Questions on Prayer*. Pendle Hill Pamphlet no. 58. Wallingford, Pa.: Pendle Hill Publications, 1951.

Hughes, Langston. "Hold Fast to Dreams." In *The Langston Hughes Reader*. New York: G. Braziller, 1958.

James, William. *The Varieties of Religious Experience*. New York: Mentor Books, 1961.

Jung, Carl G. *The Development of Personality*. Vol. 17, *Collected Works*. Princeton, N.J.: Princeton University Press, 1985.

———. *Psychology and Religion*. New Haven: Yale University Press, 1966.

——— *Two Essays on Analytical Psychology*. Princeton, N.J.: Princeton University Press, 1902.

———. *The Undiscovered Self*. Boston: Atlantic-Little, Brown, 1958.

Kelly, Thomas. *The Eternal Promise*. 2d ed. Richmond, Ind.: Friends United Press, 1988.

Kierkegaard, Søren. *Purity of Heart*. New York: Harper & Brothers, 1948.

Kunkel, Fritz. *In Search of Maturity*. New York: Charles Scribner's Sons, 1943.

Lame Deer, John, and Richard Erdoes. *Lame Deer, Seeker of Visions*. New York: Simon and Schuster, 1972.

Lewis, C. S. *Letters to Malcolm: Chiefly on Prayer*. New York: Harcourt, Brace, and World, 1963, 1964.

McGee, John. *Reality and Prayer*. New York: Harper and Row, 1957.

Merton, Thomas. *Contemplation in a World of Action*. Garden City, N.Y.: Image Books, 1923.

———. *New Seeds of Contemplation*. New York: New Directions Books, 1972.

———. *The Seven Story Mountain*. New York: New American Library Paperback, 1963.

Michaelsen, Robert S., and Wade Clark Roof, eds. *Liberal Protestantism: Realities and Possibilities*. New York: Pilgrim Press, 1986.

Miller, Samuel. *The Life of the Soul*. New York: Harper and Brothers, 1951.

Neilhardt, John. *Black Elk Speaks*. Lincoln, Neb.: University of Nebraska Press, 1979.

Niebuhr, H. Richard. *Radical Monotheism and Western Culture*. New York: Harper and Row, 1960.

Nouwen, Henri J. *Pray to Live*. Notre Dame, Ind.: Fides/Claretian, 1972.

Ornstein, Robert E. *The Psychology of Consciousness*. New York: Viking Press, 1972.

Peck, M. Scott. *A Different Drum: Community Making and Peace.* New York: Simon & Schuster, Inc., 1987.

Progoff, Ira, *At an Intensive Journal Workshop.* New York: Dialogue House Library, 1975.

Reik, Theodore. *Listening with the Third Ear.* New York: Grove Press, 1948.

Richards, M. C. *Centering, In Pottery, Poetry, and the Person.* Middletown, Conn.: Wesleyan University Press, 1964.

Rilke, Rainer Maria. *Duino Elegies and the Sonnets to Orpheus.* Translated by A. Poulin, Jr. Boston: Houghton Mifflin, 1977.

Roberts, David E. *Psychotherapy and a Christian View of Man.* New York: Charles Scribner's Sons, 1950.

Roof, Wade Clark, and William McKinney. *American Mainline Religion.* New Brunswick: Rutgers University Press, 1987.

Sanford, John A. *Dreams: God's Forgotten Language.* Philadelphia: J. B. Lippincott Co., 1968.

———. *Jesus, Paul, and Depth Psychology.* King of Prussia, Pa.: Religious Publishing House, 1974.

Sheed, F. J., trans. *The Confessions of St. Augustine.* New York: Sheed and Ward, 1951.

Teilhard de Chardin, Pierre. *The Divine Milieu.* New York: Harper & Row, 1960.

———. *The Phenomenon of Man.* New York: Harper and Row, 1975.

Teresa of Avila. *The Interior Castle.* Translated by E. Allison Peers. Garden City, N.J.: Doubleday Image Books, 1961.

Ulanov, Ann and Barry. *Religion and the Unconscious.* Philadelphia: Westminster Press, 1975.

Underhill, Evelyn. *The Mystics of the Church.* New York: George H. Doran, 1926.

———. *The School of Charity.* New York: David McKay, 1934.

van der Post, Laurens, *Jung and the Story of Our Time.* New York: Vintage Books, 1977.

Waters, John. *The Man Who Killed The Deer.* Chicago: Swallow Press, 1970.

Webber, George. *God's Colony in Man's World.* New York: Abingdon Press, 1960.

Weil, Simone. *Waiting for God.* New York: G. P. Putnam's Sons, 1951.

Williams, Charles, ed. *The Letters of Evelyn Underhill.* New York: Longmans Green, 1953.

Winter, Gibson. *The New Creation as Metropolis.* New York: Macmillan, 1963.

Wordsworth, William. "The World Is Too Much With Us." In *Masterpieces of Religious Verse.* Edited by James Dalton Morrison. New York: Harper and Row, 1948.

Wuthnow, Robert. *The Restructuring of American Religion.* Princeton, N.J.: Princeton University Press, 1988.

Additional Reading

Church of the Savior

Cosby, Gordon. *Handbook for Mission Groups.* Waco, Tex.: Word Books, 1975.
O'Connor, Elizabeth. *Eighth Day of Creation: Gifts and Creativity.* Waco, Tex: Word Books, 1971.
———. *Journey Inward, Journey Outward.* New York: Harper and Row, 1968.
———. *Our Many Selves.* New York: Harper and Row, 1971.
———. *Search for Silence.* Waco, Tex.: Word Books, 1972.

Dreams

Clift, Jean Dalby, and Wallace B. Clift. *Symbols of Transformation in Dreams.* New York: Crossroad Publishing Co., 1986.
Mahoney, Maria F. *The Meaning in Dreams and Dreaming.* Secaucus, N.J.: Citadel Press, 1966.

Human Nature, Sin, and the Shadow

Fromm, Erich. *The Anatomy of Human Destructiveness.* New York, Chicago, San Francisco: Holt, Rinehart and Winston, 1973.
Jung, C. G. *Memories, Dreams, Reflections.* New York: Random House, Vintage Books, 1963.
———. *Modern Man in Search of a Soul.* New York: Harvest Books, Harcourt, Brace & World, 1933.
Menninger, Karl, M.D. *Whatever Became of Sin?* New York: Hawthorne Books, 1973.
Niebuhr, Reinhold. *Human Nature.* Vol. 1, *The Nature and Destiny of Man.* New York: Charles Scribner's Sons, 1964.

181

————. *Human Destiny.* Vol. 2, *The Nature and Destiny of Man.* New York: Charles Scribner's Sons, 1964.

————. *The Self and the Dramas of History.* New York: Charles Scribner's Sons, 1955.

Sanford, John A. *Evil: The Shadow Side of Reality.* New York: Crossroads, 1989.

Prayer, Contemplation, and Meditation

Bailey, Raymond. *Thomas Merton on Mysticism.* Garden City, N.Y.: Doubleday and Co., Image Books, 1976.

Brother Lawrence of the Resurrection. *The Practice of the Presence of God.* Translated by John J. Delaney. Garden City, N.Y.: Doubleday and Co., Image Books, 1977.

Coburn, John B. *A Life to Live—A Way to Pray.* New York: Seabury Press, 1973.

Goleman, Daniel. *The Varieties of the Meditative Experience.* New York: Irvington Publishers, 1978.

LeShan, Lawrence. *How to Meditate.* Boston, Mass.: Bantam, 1975.

Merton, Thomas. *Contemplation in a World of Action.* Garden City, N.Y.: Doubleday and Co., Image Books, 1973.

————. *Contemplative Prayer.* Garden City, N.Y.: Doubleday and Co., Image Books, 1971.

————. *New Seeds of Contemplation.* New York: New Directions Books, 1972.

Nouwen, Henri J. *Reaching Out.* Garden City, N.Y.: Doubleday & Co., 1975.

————. *Thomas Merton: Contemplative Critic.* Notre Dame, Ind.: Fides/Claretian, 1972.

Phillips, Dorothy Berkley, Elizabeth Boyden Howes, and Lucille M. Nixon. *The Choice is Always Ours.* San Francisco: Harpers, 1989.

Wuellner, Flora Slosson. *Prayer and Our Bodies.* Nashville, Tenn.: Upper Room, 1987.

Yungblut, John R. *Rediscovering Prayer.* New York: Seabury Press, 1972.

Index